CAUGHT UP

A Biblical Theology of the Rapture

Dr. Tracy Benningfield

DEDICATION

To the Bride of Christ —

May your heart remain expectant, your lamp burning, and your eyes fixed on the eastern sky.

And to the One who is coming quickly…

This work is for You.

Even so, come, Lord Jesus.

ACKNOWLEDGEMENTS

Writing this book has been both a labor of study and a journey of the heart. I am deeply grateful to those who walked with me through the process — with prayer, support, and unwavering encouragement.

To my family: Thank you for your love, patience, and belief in the calling God placed on my life. You have given me strength in every season.

To the churches, ministries, and believers I've had the honor of serving alongside — your hunger for truth and your faithfulness in ministry have inspired every page of this work.

To the men and women of God who've gone before — pastors, scholars, and teachers who held fast to Scripture even when it cost them much — your legacy still speaks.

And most importantly, to the Holy Spirit — the true Teacher. This book is the fruit of your illumination and grace. Without You, there is no understanding, no message, and no hope.

Soli Deo gloria.

To God alone be the glory.

ABOUT THE AUTHOR

T. L. Benningfield is a seasoned pastor, theologian, missionary, and church planter with a heart deeply rooted in the Word of God and a passion for equipping the Body of Christ. Holding advanced theological degrees, including a Doctor of Ministry (D.Min.), Doctor of Divinity (D.Div.), Master of Divinity (M.Div.), and an MBA, he brings both academic depth and pastoral insight to every page he writes.

Over the years, he has served as a Senior Pastor, launched thriving ministries at home and abroad, and discipled countless believers through teaching, preaching, and leadership development. His calling is to help others understand God's Word in a way that is both doctrinally sound and spiritually transformational.

In *Caught Up: A Biblical Theology of the Rapture*, Benningfield draws from decades of study and frontline ministry experience to walk readers through one of the most important and often misunderstood doctrines of the Christian faith. Grounded in Scripture, shaped by prayer, and written with pastoral clarity, his work is a call to be informed, awake, and ready for the return of Christ.

When he's not writing or teaching, T. L. Benningfield is continuing his mission to serve the Church and proclaim the hope of the Gospel, until the trumpet sounds.

TABLE OF CONTENTS

Introduction

Why the Rapture Matters: Not Escapism, But Eschatology

"Therefore, encourage one another with these words."

— 1 Thessalonians 4:18

There is a sound coming. It's not audible yet to human ears, but it is approaching with every heartbeat of history. One day soon, a trumpet will blast, a shout will ring out, and in an instant—*in the twinkling of an eye*—millions of people will vanish. Not abducted. Not erased. But **caught up**, just as Scripture says, taken to meet the Lord in the air. This event is not fiction. It's not religious poetry. It's not a metaphor for death or a symbol of hope. It is a literal, supernatural, and imminent promise made by the Lord Jesus Himself. And it matters—now more than ever.

This book is about that event, what the Bible teaches about it, and why the Church must once again take it seriously. The Rapture isn't spiritual escapism. It's not a fringe theory for the speculative or the fearful. It is a critical aspect of biblical eschatology—tied directly to God's redemptive plans for Israel, His judgments upon the nations,

1

and His glorification of the Church. In an age marked by confusion, mockery, apostasy, and doctrinal drift, there is a desperate need for clarity on what the Rapture is and what it is not.

Some critics object to the idea by saying, "The word 'rapture' isn't in the Bible." That's partially true. The English word "rapture" does not appear in our Bibles, but the Greek word *harpazō* most certainly does. In 1 Thessalonians 4:17, Paul describes believers being "caught up" to meet the Lord in the air. The Greek term for "caught up" is *harpazō*, which means to seize, to snatch away suddenly and forcefully. When the Bible was translated into Latin (the *Vulgate*), *harpazō* became rapiemur, from the root **rapturo**, which is where the English word "rapture" comes from. So, while the word "rapture" is English shorthand, the concept is deeply and firmly biblical.

A key truth we will unpack is that the Rapture is distinct from the Second Coming of Christ. These are not two names for the same event, but two stages of one grand return. The Rapture involves Christ coming *to meet His Church* in the clouds. The Second Coming involves Christ returning *with* His Church, in power and glory, to execute judgment on a rebellious world. The first is sudden, invisible to the world, and comforting to the Church. The second is visible, triumphant, and terrifying to the wicked.

Sadly, the Rapture has been misunderstood and misrepresented. Many believers today are skeptical or even dismissive of it. Some have been disillusioned by sensationalists who tried to set dates or predict world events with their own brand of theology. Others have absorbed symbolic or allegorical methods of interpretation that blur the distinctions between Israel and the Church. Still others have simply never been taught to take Bible prophecy seriously.

This book does not seek to sensationalize or oversimplify.

Instead, it will take a reverent, Scripture-heavy approach to explore the biblical theology of the Rapture and to fairly, yet critically, test various rapture views. While we affirm the Pre- Tribulation Rapture view, we do not arrive at it casually or mindlessly. Instead, we will demonstrate how it aligns with the full sweep of Scripture—both the Old and New Testaments, and with the prophetic patterns established by God throughout redemptive history.

We will examine why Israel and the Church must be seen as distinct peoples with distinct roles in God's prophetic timetable. We will explore the 70 Weeks prophecy of Daniel and its significance for Israel's future. We will look at Paul's letters, Jesus' words in the Olivet Discourse, and the apocalyptic imagery of Revelation. We will also interact with key voices across church history—from the early Church Fathers to modern theologians—both those who supported and those who challenged this view. Most importantly, we will let Scripture interpret Scripture.

The Rapture is not just about escape. It is about preparation. It is not about fear, but hope. Paul wrote that believers should "encourage one another with these words" (1 Thess. 4:18). The doctrine of the Rapture is meant to give the Church boldness in its witness, holiness in its living, and joy in its waiting. It reminds us that we are not appointed to wrath, but to salvation (1 Thess. 5:9). It assures us that God finishes what He starts—that Christ will come again, not just to reign, but to receive His Bride (John 14:1-3).

In the chapters ahead, we will journey from the etymology of *harpazō* to the eschatological framework of Daniel. We will contrast the Rapture with the Second Coming, dive into 2 Thessalonians and the mystery of the Restrainer, and walk through Revelation's judgments to see what happens after the Church is caught up. Along the way, we will also explore how current cultural trends—the rise of apostasy, gender confusion, lawlessness, and spiritual deception—mirror the prophetic warnings given for the "days of Noah" and the "last days."

This isn't just a theological exploration. It is a call to wake up, to watch, and to live ready. Christ is coming. And He's coming sooner than the world thinks.

Chapter 1

Harpazō: Caught Up With Christ

"Then we who are alive and remain shall be caught up together with them in the clouds to meet the Lord in the air. And thus we shall always be with the Lord."

— 1 Thessalonians 4:17

When the Apostle Paul wrote to the church in Thessalonica, he wasn't offering them theology in a vacuum. He was writing as a pastor, a shepherd, a father in the faith, responding to a deeply emotional and unsettling crisis within the young church. Some believers had died. Others were confused. Many feared that those who had passed away would somehow miss the return of Christ and be separated from the eternal glory promised to His saints. Paul, inspired by the Holy Spirit, didn't leave them to speculation. He offered something concrete, a doctrine wrapped in comfort, something solid, something supernatural. He offered them the promise of the *harpazō*, the catching up.

That word—*caught up*—is not minor, nor is it symbolic.

It is a thunderclap of hope in the middle of human grief. Paul writes not merely to ease their sorrow but to anchor it in truth. He does not tell them to remember the good times or celebrate life; he tells them that Christ Himself will descend from heaven, and that the dead in Christ will rise first. Then, he says, "we who are alive and remain shall be caught up together with them… to meet the Lord in the air."

This is not myth. This is not metaphor. This is a prophetic promise. And it demands our attention.

The Word "Rapture": Rooted in Scripture

One of the most common objections to the doctrine of the Rapture is the claim that the word itself never appears in the Bible. On the surface, that's true. If you search for the word "rapture" in your English Bible, you won't find it. But this objection collapses the moment you examine the original language. In 1 Thessalonians 4:17, the Apostle Paul uses the Greek word **harpazō**, which means "to seize suddenly," "to snatch away by force," "to rescue," or "to remove quickly and decisively." This is not a passive word. It conveys urgency, power, and intentionality.

We find *harpazō* used throughout the New Testament to describe similar supernatural removals:

- In Acts 8:39, Philip is "caught up" by the Spirit and is instantly transported.

- In 2 Corinthians 12:2, Paul says he was "caught up" to the third heaven.

- In Revelation 12:5, the male child is "caught up" to God and His throne.

This same word—*harpazō*—is what Paul uses in 1 Thessalonians to describe the Church's sudden removal from earth to meet Christ in the air. When the New Testament was later translated into Latin (in the *Vulgate*), the word *harpazō* became rapiemur, derived from the root rapturo, which is where we derive the English word "rapture."

So, while "rapture" is not an English Bible term, it is a biblical concept firmly embedded in the Greek and Latin translations of Paul's inspired letters. To deny the Rapture on the basis of vocabulary is to miss the clear and consistent teaching of Scripture.

A Word for the Weary: The Pastoral Purpose Behind the Rapture

It's crucial to remember the context of Paul's words in 1 Thessalonians 4. He wasn't writing a doctrinal treatise for the sake of theological debate. He was writing to believers who were worried, confused, and grieving. Their concern was intensely practical: *what happens to believers who die before Christ returns?*

Paul doesn't rebuke them for asking. He doesn't dismiss their emotions. Instead, he gives them something far better than speculation—he gives them revelation.

He writes, "I do not want you to be uninformed, brothers, about those who are asleep, that you may not grieve as others who have no hope." Then he lays out a precise sequence of events, meant not to scare them, but to encourage them:

"The Lord Himself will descend from heaven with a shout, with the voice of an archangel, and with the trumpet of God. The dead in Christ will rise first. Then we who are alive and remain will be caught up…"

—   1 Thessalonians 4:16-17

This was a new revelation, a mystery now made clear.

Paul doesn't suggest that believers "go to heaven when they die" in some abstract spiritual state. He teaches something far more dramatic and physical: a bodily resurrection of the dead, followed by the instant transformation of the living.

And all of it concludes with the most comforting phrase possible:

"So shall we ever be with the Lord."

The Rapture Sequence: Step by Step

Paul's words in 1 Thessalonians 4:13-18 and 1 Corinthians 15:51-54 offer a detailed, chronological picture of the Rapture. This is not vague imagery; it is a divinely inspired outline:

1. **Christ descends from heaven** — not spiritually, not symbolically, but bodily.

2. **A shout, a voice, and a trumpet blast** accompany His arrival.

3. **The dead in Christ are raised** — believers who have died will receive glorified bodies.

4. **Living believers are transformed and caught up**—a sudden

metamorphosis from mortality to immortality.

5. **We meet the Lord in the air**, not on the ground, not in heaven, but in the sky.

6. **We remain with Him forever** — eternal union begins here.

This is consistent with Jesus' own promise in John 14:3: *"I will come again and receive you to Myself, that where I am, you may be also."*

Parallel Truth:
The Mystery Revealed in 1 Corinthians 15

Paul expands upon this doctrine in his first letter to the Corinthians. In chapter 15, verses 51–52, he says:

"Behold! I tell you a mystery. We shall not all sleep, but we shall all be changed, in a moment, in the twinkling of an eye…"

Here, Paul emphasizes both the speed and the universality of this event. It will not be a process—it will be instantaneous. It will not happen only to the dead—it will include the living. The corruptible will put on incorruption. The mortal will be clothed in immortality.

And once again, Paul doesn't end with speculation. He ends with a celebration:

"Death is swallowed up in victory… thanks be to God who gives us the victory through our Lord Jesus Christ!"

For believers, the Rapture is not an escape from hardship. It is the consummation of our victory in Christ.

Is the Rapture the Same as the Second Coming?

Many believers today confuse the Rapture with the Second Coming of Christ, treating them as one and the same event. But Scripture distinguishes them in multiple key ways.

Consider the following contrasts:

Rapture	Second Coming
Christ comes **for** His Church	Christ returns **with** His Church
Happens **in the air**	Happens **on the earth** (Zechariah 14:4)
A **blessing** for believers	A **judgment** upon the world
Imminent—no signs needed	**Preceded** by specific signs (Matt. 24)
Seen only by the Church	**Visible to all** (Revelation 1:7)
Results in the Church going **to** heaven	Results in Christ setting up His kingdom on earth

These are not minor differences. They point to two distinct phases of the return of Christ:

- First, the Rapture — sudden, joyful, hidden, for His Bride.

- Then, the Second Coming — glorious, visible, and with judgment, as the King of Kings returns to conquer.

The implications of this doctrine are profound. If Christ is coming at any moment to catch up His Church, how should we live?

Paul gives several answers throughout his letters:

- **Holiness** – "He who has this hope in him purifies himself" (1 John 3:3)

- **Urgency** – "Now is our salvation nearer than when we believed" (Romans 13:11)

- **Watchfulness** – "Let us not sleep as others do, but let us watch and be sober" (1 Thess. 5:6)

- **Encouragement** – "Comfort one another with these words" (1 Thess. 4:18)

- **Faithfulness** – "Be steadfast… always abounding in the work of the Lord" (1 Cor. 15:58)

The Rapture is not merely theology for the mind—it is fuel for the soul. It is the doctrine that tells us: *This world is not our home. This moment is not the end. Our Redeemer is coming— soon.*

Not Appointed to Wrath

One of the most significant implications of the Rapture is its role in delivering the Church from divine judgment. Paul makes this clear in 1 Thessalonians 1:10 and 5:9:

> *"…Jesus, who delivers us from the wrath to come." "For God has not appointed us to wrath, but to obtain salvation…"*

The period of divine wrath, known as the Tribulation, is described in Revelation chapters 6–19. This time of judgment is aimed at an unbelieving world and the rebellious nations, not at the Church, which has already been justified in Christ.

Just as God removed Noah before the flood and Lot before the fire, so too He will remove His Bride before the outpouring of wrath. The harpazō is not just an escape; it is a pattern of divine protection consistent throughout Scripture.

Chapter 2

The Spectrum of Views: From Church Fathers to Modern Debate

"The coming of the Lord has always been near in every generation—awaited, watched for, and longed after. And now more than ever, the signs multiply, but so do the interpretations."

The doctrine of the Rapture, though rooted in clear biblical language, has traveled a complex road through Church history. Over time, it has been viewed with expectancy, confusion, rejection, resurgence, and again division. To understand where we stand today, we must look at where we came from—not because history defines truth, but because it helps us see why the Church has taken different paths over the centuries.

This chapter surveys that landscape. It is not meant to give final answers—that is the work of Scripture, not history— but it will show how serious students of the Bible have wrestled with the timing, nature, and meaning of Christ's return.

Importantly, it will also demonstrate how shifts in worldview, theology, and even political events have influenced views of the

Rapture and the end times.

The Early Church: Watching, Waiting, Suffering

In the earliest generations after the apostles, the Church was united in one conviction: **Jesus is coming back—and soon**. The writings of the Apostolic Fathers (100–300 AD) reveal a Church that yearned for the return of Christ and anticipated it at any moment.

Church leaders such as Irenaeus, Justin Martyr, and Papias affirmed a literal return of Christ, a future millennial kingdom, and a time of tribulation preceding it. While they didn't use modern terms like "pre-trib" or "post-trib," they clearly expected a bodily resurrection and return.

Perhaps the clearest early reference to something resembling a Rapture comes from Pseudo-Ephraim, a 4th- or 6th- century text that says:

"All the saints and elect of God are gathered together before the tribulation... and are taken to the Lord lest they see the confusion that is to overwhelm the world."

While this isn't ironclad "proof" of a pre-tribulation rapture in early theology, it does suggest that the idea of a rescue before wrath existed long before modern dispensationalism.

The early Church, though under intense persecution, did not allegorize Christ's return. They expected it. They lived as if it could happen at any moment.

From Literalism to Allegory: Augustine and the Rise of Amillennialism

By the 4th century, Christianity had moved from the margins to the empire. With Constantine's conversion and the institutionalization of the Church, the persecuted remnant had become the imperial religion. And with that cultural shift came a theological one.

The dominant voice in this new era was Augustine of Hippo (354–430 AD). Though brilliant and deeply influential, Augustine introduced a system of interpretation that would reshape eschatology for over a millennium: allegorical interpretation.

Augustine argued that:

- The "millennium" of Revelation 20 was symbolic of the Church Age

- Christ's reign was spiritual, not future or earthly

- The Church had replaced Israel in God's plan

This view became known as amillennialism—the belief that there is no literal 1,000-year reign of Christ to come, and that the events of Revelation are largely symbolic or already fulfilled. It dominated Catholic theology, and later much of Reformed theology as well.

In this view, the idea of a distinct Rapture was essentially lost. The second coming became one singular event—no distinction between Christ coming for His Church and coming in judgment. Over time, much of the Church stopped expecting Christ and instead focused on building Christendom on earth.

Reformation and Return to Scripture

The Protestant Reformation in the 16th century reclaimed several core doctrines, including justification by faith, the authority of Scripture, and salvation by grace. But it did not immediately restore biblical eschatology. Reformers like Martin Luther and John Calvin, while brilliant in soteriology, retained many of Augustine's eschatological assumptions, including amillennialism.

However, a seed was planted—the principle of *sola scriptura* (Scripture alone). As the Bible became more available to ordinary believers, questions about prophecy and the end times re-emerged. Believers began to read Revelation, Daniel, and Paul's letters with fresh eyes. Some began to ask: *Is there more than one phase to Christ's return? Is the Church the same as Israel? Could Jesus come back at any moment?*

These questions would find new traction in the centuries that followed.

Rise of Futurism and the Recovery of Israel

By the 17th and 18th centuries, some Bible scholars began challenging amillennial assumptions. Catholic Jesuit Francisco Ribera (late 1500s) proposed a futurist view—that Revelation describes future events, not just historical allegory. Though his motives were mixed (he intended to counter Reformation accusations that the Pope was the Antichrist), his ideas planted the foundation for futurism, the belief that Bible prophecy—especially the Tribulation, Antichrist, and return of Christ—**is** yet future.

This approach re-opened the door to a literal reading of:

- Daniel's 70th Week (Daniel 9)

- Israel's national restoration

- The idea of a future Great Tribulation

- A literal millennial reign of Christ

The 19th Century: Dispensationalism and the Pre-Trib Rapture

The most significant turning point came in the early 1800s, when John Nelson Darby, a British theologian and key figure in the Plymouth Brethren movement, systematized what became known as dispensationalism.

Darby's contributions were immense:

- He emphasized a literal interpretation of prophecy

- He distinguished between Israel and the Church

- He taught that the Rapture would occur before the Tribulation

- He laid out a clear prophetic timeline, consistent with a futurist reading

This view spread rapidly, especially in the English-speaking world, through:

- The Scofield Reference Bible (1909)

- The Dallas Theological Seminary

- Teachers like Lewis Sperry Chafer, Charles Ryrie, and John Walvoord

By the mid-20th century, the Pre-Tribulation Rapture became the dominant view among evangelical and fundamentalist churches in the U.S., especially during the Cold War era.

20th–21st Century: Resurgence, Criticism, and Confusion

While the Pre-Trib view gained popularity in the West, it also faced increasing criticism. Some argued it was a recent innovation. Others accused it of promoting escapism. Still others favored Post-Tribulation or Pre-Wrath views that placed the Rapture closer to or within the Tribulation itself.

Prominent voices emerged on each side:

- George Eldon Ladd popularized the Post-Tribulation Rapture

- Marv Rosenthal developed the Pre-Wrath Rapture position.

- Tim LaHaye brought Pre-Trib ideas into popular culture with the *Left Behind* series (A series that was suggested to Tim by Shirey

Peters, the Wife of Dr. Art Peters, who was my mentor for several years in early pastoral ministry).

- Scholars like Craig Blomberg, N.T. Wright, and R.C. Sproul pushed back with either symbolic or partial preterist readings of prophecy.

In recent decades, even many evangelical churches have quietly dropped eschatology altogether, deeming it too divisive or mysterious. Meanwhile, a resurgence of Reformed Theology has reintroduced amillennialism and covenantal replacement of Israel into the mainstream.

The Four Main Views Today

While variations exist, most Rapture positions today fall into one of four categories:

1. Pre-Tribulation – Rapture occurs *before* the 7-year Tribulation.

2. Mid-Tribulation – Rapture occurs *midway* through the Tribulation.

3. Post-Tribulation – Rapture occurs *at the end*, just before the Second Coming

4. Pre-Wrath – Rapture occurs *before God's wrath*, after much of the Tribulation.

Each view is an attempt to synthesize the biblical data, but only one holds together Scripture, pattern, and prophetic integrity most consistently. That is the view we will explore, test, and affirm in this book: the Pre-Tribulation Rapture.

Where History Leads Us

The history of Rapture theology is not the source of our doctrine, but it is the backdrop. What we see is that the expectation of Christ's imminent return has never fully disappeared, even if it was obscured for a time. Every major resurgence in biblical fidelity—whether in the early church, the Reformation, or the modern evangelical movement—has been accompanied by a renewed longing for the return of Christ.

We believe that longing is not only healthy, it is biblical. As we move forward, we will not argue from tradition. We will argue from Scripture, guided by the Spirit, and always with this goal in mind:

"To comfort and encourage one another with these words."

Chapter 3

The Restrainer Removed: The Spirit and the Church

"For the mystery of lawlessness is already at work; only He who now restrains will do so until He is taken out of the way."

— 2 Thessalonians 2:7

The apostle Paul wrote with clarity. He wrote with purpose. But sometimes, he wrote with a divine sense of restraint, revealing enough truth to stir the Church's understanding, while concealing just enough to provoke careful discernment. One of the most theologically rich and prophetically urgent examples of this is found in 2 Thessalonians 2, where Paul speaks of a force—more precisely, a Person—who is holding back the rise of lawlessness in the world. This individual is described as the restrainer, and Paul tells us that once this restrainer is "taken out of the way," the world will change forever. The man of sin—the Antichrist—will be revealed, and the prophetic clock of judgment will begin to chime.

But who is this restrainer? And what does it mean for him to be "taken out of the way"? More pointedly, how does this passage relate to the doctrine of the Rapture?

The answers to these questions are not only fascinating— they are foundational. Because if the restrainer is the Holy Spirit working through the Church, and if He is removed before the revealing of the Antichrist, then the Rapture must come before the Tribulation. In this chapter, we explore this critical truth.

A Church in Confusion

Paul's second letter to the Thessalonians was not theoretical. It was deeply pastoral. The early Church had received rich teaching about the coming of Christ. Paul had already written to them in 1 Thessalonians about the Rapture— that moment when believers would be "caught up" to meet the Lord in the air (1 Thess. 4:17). But confusion had crept in. False teachers had begun to spread the idea that the Day of the Lord— the period of God's judgment and wrath—had already begun (2 Thess. 2:2). This unsettled many believers. Some feared they had missed the Rapture. Others were confused about the prophetic timeline.

Paul responded not with speculation, but with inspired revelation. He tells them that two events must occur before the Day of the Lord arrives:

1. A great apostasy or falling away from the faith.

2. The revealing of "the man of lawlessness," commonly understood to be the Antichrist.

And then Paul drops a mysterious insight: the Antichrist cannot be revealed yet, because something—or someone—is restraining him.

"And now you know what is restraining him, that he may be revealed in his own time."

— (2 Thess. 2:6)

This is a spiritual mystery embedded in a prophetic timeline.

The Mystery of Lawlessness and the One Who Restrains

Paul describes a powerful force at work in the world—a "mystery of lawlessness" that is already operating behind the scenes. This is the same spirit that John described as "the spirit of antichrist" (1 John 4:3), and it is active in every generation. But Paul tells us it is being restrained. Something is keeping this lawlessness from flooding the world. More than that, someone is preventing the Antichrist from stepping onto the stage before his appointed time.

The Greek word Paul uses for "restrain" is katechō, meaning to hold down, suppress, or restrain by force. And interestingly, Paul shifts his grammatical terms:

- In verse 6, he uses a neuter participle: *to katechon* ("what restrains")

- In verse 7, he switches to a masculine: *ho katechōn* ("he who restrains")

This shift indicates a personal being who also manifests through impersonal means or roles. The restrainer is not simply an institution or abstract force. He is someone with agency, power, and divine authority.

Who Is the Restrainer?

Throughout church history, scholars have offered various theories about the identity of the restrainer:

- Some have said it is human government, particularly the Roman Empire.

- Others have pointed to Michael the Archangel, as described in Daniel 10 and 12.

- Still others have argued it refers to the Church, Christ's body on earth.

- But the view that aligns best with the text, theology, and timing is that the Restrainer is the Holy Spirit, specifically the Spirit's presence through the Church in this age.

This interpretation explains both the neuter and masculine grammatical forms. The Holy Spirit (pneuma, neuter in Greek) operates invisibly and universally, yet He is also a divine Person (He who restrains). He works through the Church, which is the temple of the Holy Spirit (1 Cor. 6:19), the dwelling place of God on earth (Eph. 2:22), and the salt and light that holds back moral decay and spiritual darkness (Matt. 5:13–14).

As long as the Church is present, the full manifestation of lawlessness is held back.

The Holy Spirit's Ministry in the Church Age

The ministry of the Holy Spirit is unique in this present age. In the Old Testament, the Spirit would come upon certain individuals—prophets, judges, kings—for specific tasks. But since the day of Pentecost (Acts 2), the Spirit now indwells every believer permanently.

This indwelling is not a mere private benefit; it is a cosmic restraint on evil. Especially if the believers are seeking to accomplish the work of Christ in the world.

Through the Church, the Spirit:

- Proclaims the truth of the gospel.

- Confronts evil and error.

- Discerns false doctrine.

- Restrains the influence of demonic agendas.

- Upholds righteousness in society.

The Church, by simply being Spirit-indwelt, functions as **a preserving force** in a world bent toward rebellion. The Holy Spirit is not restraining evil from the sidelines. He is doing it through His people—redeemed, sealed, and commissioned.

What Does It Mean to Be "Taken Out of the Way"?

Paul says the restrainer "will continue to restrain until He is taken out of the way." The phrase does not mean that the Holy Spirit ceases to exist or is withdrawn from the earth entirely. The Spirit is eternal and omnipresent. Even during the Tribulation, the Spirit will be active in saving, sealing, and empowering those who come to Christ—such as the 144,000 Jewish witnesses and the multitude of Tribulation saints (Rev. 7:9–17).

But what does change is His role as restrainer through the Church. When the Rapture occurs, and the Church is caught up to meet Christ in the air, the Spirit's restraining ministry through believers is also removed. It is the removal of the temple, not the presence. The temple—the Church—is no longer on earth. And thus, the world is suddenly void of its greatest spiritual resistance.

The Rapture Precedes the Antichrist

This connection is critical: the removal of the restrainer must precede the revealing of the Antichrist.

Paul is precise:

- The man of lawlessness will be revealed **only after** the restrainer is taken out of the way (2 Thess. 2:8)

- Then, and only then, will the world be plunged into deception and strong delusion (2 Thess. 2:11)

- And only at the Second Coming will Christ destroy the Antichrist with "the breath of His mouth" (2 Thess. 2:8)

If the restrainer is the Spirit through the Church, then the Church must be removed first. This aligns perfectly with the Pre- Tribulation Rapture view.

Why This Matters: A Spiritual Collapse After the Rapture

Once the Church is taken, the world will undergo a moral and spiritual collapse unlike anything it has seen. The disappearance of millions of Spirit-filled believers will not only shock the globe—it will remove the last line of defense against global lawlessness.

There will be:

- No gospel-preaching churches to confront deception.

- No Holy Spirit-filled voices to resist rising evil.

- No Christlike salt to preserve righteousness in culture.

- No bride to reflect the image of the bridegroom.

It is no coincidence that immediately after the restrainer is removed, the Antichrist rises to power (Rev. 6:1–2). The Rapture clears the way for his ascent.

God's Pattern: Removal Before Wrath

Throughout Scripture, God has demonstrated a clear pattern: He removes the righteous before unleashing judgment.

- **Noah** was lifted in the ark before the flood fell.

- **Lot** was escorted out of Sodom before fire rained down.

- **Enoch** was taken before the judgment of the flood.

- **Rahab** was sheltered before Jericho collapsed.

Jesus Himself said:

> *"As it was in the days of Noah... as it was in the days of Lot... so it will be in the day when the Son of Man is revealed."*

> — Luke 17:26–30

This consistent pattern testifies to God's mercy. He does not pour out His wrath upon His people. The Church is not appointed to wrath (1 Thess. 5:9), and it will not face the hour of testing that will come upon the whole world (Rev. 3:10). The restrainer must be removed. The Church must be caught up. And only then does judgment begin.

Living as Restrainers Until That Day

Until that moment, we have a mission. The Church is not meant to merely watch for the Rapture; we are meant to restrain until the trumpet sounds.

That means:

- Standing for truth in a culture of lies

- Shining light in an age of confusion

- Loving our enemies, preaching the gospel, and making disciples

- Occupying until He comes (Luke 19:13)

The Spirit of God is not passive within you. He is a warrior.

A witness. A fire. He is the restrainer who holds back lawlessness—not by force, but through holiness, love, and truth.

The Time Is Short

The mystery of lawlessness is no longer hidden. We see its effects every day: the distortion of truth, the exaltation of sin, the global systems preparing for control, deception, and collapse. But it is still being held back.

For now.

When the restrainer is removed, the floodgates will open. The world will plunge headlong into its final rebellion. But before that happens, the Bride will be called home. The Church will be caught up. And the Holy Spirit's restraining ministry through the Body of Christ will be complete.

Until that trumpet sounds, we restrain. We preach. We shine. We wait. And we hope.

"He who now restrains will do so until He is taken out of the way."

Then the end will begin.

Chapter 4

The Last Trumpet: Rapture and Resurrection in Paul's Letters

"In a moment, in the twinkling of an eye, at the last trumpet… the dead will be raised incorruptible, and we shall be changed."

— 1 Corinthians 15:52

There are a few passages in the New Testament that shimmer with as much mystery, majesty, and expectation as Paul's words about the resurrection of the dead. These aren't abstract theological ideas. They are promises—sure, physical, personal promises—meant to fill believers with comfort, courage, and anticipation. And at the heart of these promises is the great hope of the Church: the Rapture.

Paul's letters to the Corinthians and Thessalonians unveil not only the mechanics of this glorious event but also its timing, its transformative power, and its theological necessity. In this chapter, we will examine two of the most vivid Rapture passages in Scripture: 1 Corinthians 15:50–58 and 1 Thessalonians 4:13– 18, drawing out their prophetic significance and doctrinal richness.

These passages describe the "last trumpet," a mysterious call from heaven, a sudden transformation of believers, and the climactic reunion between the Church and her Lord. For many, these verses are poetic. For the believer, they are prophetic. They are God's divine interruption in human history—when the mortal puts on immortality, and faith finally becomes sight.

A Letter to a Confused Church

When Paul wrote to the Corinthians, he was addressing a Church rich in spiritual gifts but poor in spiritual maturity. They were a Church caught up in controversies, questions, and cultural compromise. Among their many confusions was a fundamental misunderstanding about the resurrection of the body.

Some in Corinth, influenced by Greek dualism, denied the physical resurrection altogether. Paul, with pastoral urgency, sets the record straight in 1 Corinthians 15. He builds his case with the historical fact of Christ's resurrection and then outlines the promise of resurrection for all believers. Near the chapter's end, he describes something unprecedented—something mystical, instantaneous, and glorious:

"Behold, I tell you a mystery: We shall not all sleep, but we shall all be changed."

— (1 Cor. 15:51)

Here, Paul introduces a divine mystery—something previously hidden but now revealed through the Spirit. Not all believers will die ("sleep"), but all will be changed. This change is not gradual. It happens "in a moment, in the twinkling of an eye," when the last trumpet sounds.

The Last Trumpet: What Is It?

The phrase "last trumpet" has caused some confusion. Some associate it with the seventh trumpet of Revelation 11, assuming a Post-Tribulational timing. But a closer study of the context reveals that Paul is not referencing Revelation at all—it hadn't even been written yet.

Instead, Paul's use of "last trumpet" draws on Old Testament typology and Roman military imagery:

- In Jewish tradition, trumpets signaled convocations, announcements, or movement (Num. 10:1–10)

- At Sinai, the trumpet of God called Israel to meet Him in holiness (Ex. 19:16–19)

- In Roman military camps, a series of trumpets governed soldier movement: the first to arise, the second to pack up, and the last trumpet to march.

In this context, the "last trumpet" is not the trumpet of judgment—it's the trumpet of gathering. It is the trumpet of completion, the final call for the Church to rise and meet her King.

Paul speaks of the same trumpet again in 1 Thessalonians:

"For the Lord Himself will descend from heaven with a shout, with the voice of the archangel, and with the trumpet of God."

— 1 Thess. 4:16

It is not the trumpet of wrath—it is the trumpet of rescue. The last trumpet signals the end of the Church's mission and the beginning of her eternal reward.

What Happens at the Last Trumpet?

The moment the trumpet sounds, two miraculous events occur simultaneously:

1. The Dead in Christ are Raised

Believers who have died—those who "sleep in Jesus"— will be resurrected in glorified bodies. This is not soul awakening; it is bodily resurrection, patterned after Christ's own resurrection body (1 Cor. 15:20–23).

2. Living Believers are Transformed

Those who are alive at the moment will not die. Instead, they will be "changed." Their mortal, corruptible bodies will be instantly transformed into immortal, incorruptible vessels fit for eternity.

Paul is emphatic:

> *"This mortal must put on immortality."*

> — (1 Cor. 15:53)

This is the culmination of salvation—not just justification or sanctification, but glorification. It is also a revelation that the existing body is corrupted and must also be redeemed in the same way the spirit of man has been redeemed.

Victory Over Death

After describing this divine transformation, Paul breaks into doxology:

"Death is swallowed up in victory."

— (1 Cor. 15:54)

The Rapture is not merely an escape from tribulation; it is the victory cry of the cross. It is the full expression of Christ's triumph over death, applied to His people. Every funeral, every grave, every tear is answered in this moment.

"O death, where is your sting? O grave, where is your victory?"

The sting of death is sin. The strength of sin is the law. But Christ has fulfilled the law, paid for sin, and conquered death. The Rapture is when that victory becomes experiential— when the Church enters into the fullness of redemption.

The Thessalonian Comfort: Not Appointed to Wrath

Paul's first letter to the Thessalonians offers a pastoral parallel to his message in Corinth. This young Church was grieving over believers who had died. Some feared they would miss Christ's return. Paul comforts them with a majestic description of the Rapture.

"The Lord Himself will descend from heaven with a shout… and the dead in Christ will rise first. Then we who are alive… shall be caught up… to meet the

Lord in the air."

— 1 Thess. 4:16–17

Paul uses the Greek word harpazō—to snatch away, seize quickly. Again, this is the origin of the Latin term "rapturo," from which we get our English word "Rapture."

He ends the passage with these words:

"Therefore comfort one another with these words."

— (1 Thess. 4:18)

Comfort. Not fear. Not dread. The Rapture is meant to encourage the Church, not terrify her.

Paul continues in Chapter 5 by warning that the Day of the Lord will come like a thief in the night—but not for the Church. Believers are not in darkness. They are "sons of the light."

Then he gives this divine assurance:

"For God did not appoint us to wrath, but to obtain salvation through our Lord Jesus Christ."

— (1 Thess. 5:9)

This is a key doctrinal anchor. The Church is not appointed to the wrath of God, which will be poured out during the Tribulation (Rev. 6–19). The Rapture delivers believers from that wrath, just as Noah was lifted before the flood, and Lot was removed before Sodom burned.

What about the Post-Tribulational View?

Some argue that Paul's use of "last trumpet" links the Rapture with the seventh trumpet in Revelation 11. But this confuses terminology with timing.

- Paul wrote 1 Corinthians around A.D. 55

- John wrote Revelation around A.D. 95

- Paul never references the trumpets of judgment in Revelation.

Moreover, the seventh trumpet in Revelation is a judgment trumpet, unleashing wrath on the earth (Rev. 11:15-19), while Paul's trumpet is a resurrection trumpet, associated with victory, joy, and transformation.

Equating the two overlooks their vastly different contexts, audiences, and purposes.

Theological Harmony with Pre-Tribulation Rapture

The passages in 1 Corinthians 15 and 1 Thessalonians 4–5 align seamlessly with the Pre-Tribulational view:

- They describe a sudden, transformative event—not preceded by cosmic judgment, but by divine preparation.

- They speak of comfort and rescue, not wrath and warning.

- They fit into Paul's larger eschatology, where the Church is delivered **before** the day of God's fury begins.

The "last trumpet" for the Church is not the end of time. It is the end of our waiting. The Church has run her race. The Bride has made herself ready. And at the sound of that trumpet, she will rise—not into chaos, but into glory.

Living in Light of the Trumpet

Paul ends 1 Corinthians 15 not with a chart, but with a charge:

"Therefore, my beloved brethren, be steadfast, immovable, always abounding in the work of the Lord, knowing that your labor is not in vain."

— (1 Cor. 15:58)

The doctrine of the Rapture is not an escape clause. It is a motivation for faithfulness.

We live in the shadow of the trumpet:

- Watching

- Working

- Waiting

- Worshiping

And when it sounds, in the twinkling of an eye, we shall be changed.

Chapter 5

Daniel's Seventieth Week: Why the Church Is Not in the Tribulation

"Seventy weeks are decreed about your people and your holy city..."

— Daniel 9:24

Every theology of the Rapture must answer one crucial question: Does the church need to be removed prior to the tribulation period? If so, why must the Church be removed before the Tribulation?

While many look to Revelation for answers—and rightly so—the clearest foundation lies not in the final book of the Bible, but in the prophetic writings of the Old Testament.

In Daniel 9, the angel Gabriel delivers to the prophet a breathtaking timeline of redemptive history. He outlines a period of "seventy weeks"—a prophetic countdown that would shape the future of Israel, Jerusalem, the Messiah, and the world. This prophecy, given during Israel's exile, is not about the Church. It is not about Gentile nations. It is explicitly about Daniel's people and Daniel's city—that is, Israel and Jerusalem.

When we understand Daniel's seventy weeks, we understand why the

Church cannot be present for the Tribulation. Because the Tribulation—what Daniel calls the 70th week—is not about the Bride of Christ. It is about God finishing His covenant dealings with Israel and judging the rebellious nations.

We have to understand that this interpretation was missed prior to May 14th 1948, because at that time Israel did not exist. As previously stated, the allegorical approach to interpretation was predominant. But after Israel became a nation again due to the atrocities of Hitler, the League of Nations, now the United Nations, gave Israel back to the Jewish people.

The Prophetic Structure: Seventy Weeks of Years

The prophecy in Daniel 9:24–27 unfolds like a divine calendar:

"Seventy weeks are decreed for your people and your holy city to finish transgression, to put an end to sin, to atone for iniquity, to bring in everlasting righteousness…"

The Hebrew word translated "weeks" is shavuim, meaning "sevens." These are not seven-day weeks but seven- year periods—a pattern already established in Leviticus 25 and understood by Jewish readers.

So:

- 70 x 7 = 490 prophetic years

Gabriel outlines a series of events:

- **7 weeks (49 years)**: Jerusalem is rebuilt.

- **62 weeks (434 years)**: Until the coming of the Messiah

- **1 week (7 years)**: A future final period of intense tribulation

The first 69 weeks (483 years) lead up to "the cutting off of the Anointed One"—the crucifixion of Jesus Christ (Dan. 9:26). This prophecy was fulfilled precisely. From the decree to rebuild Jerusalem (444 B.C.) to the ministry of Jesus, and subsequent death of Jesus in Christ (c. A.D. 33), exactly 483 years elapsed.

Then—suddenly—the prophetic clock stops.

The 70th week has not yet occurred.

The Pause: A Mystery Age Begins

The gap between the 69th and 70th week is not a miscalculation— it's a mystery revealed in the New Testament. This is the Church Age, a parenthetical season in which God extends salvation to all nations through the gospel. Paul calls this a mystery hidden for ages but now revealed (Eph. 3:4–6).

- The Church is not Israel

- The Church is not a continuation of the Old Covenant

- The Church is a new creation (2 Cor. 5:17), formed by the Spirit, composed of Jew and Gentile alike.

This age was not revealed to Daniel, but it is foundational to understanding why the Church must be removed before the 70th week resumes. Because the 70th week is not about the Church— it is about finishing the covenant work God promised to Israel.

The 70th Week: The Tribulation Period

Daniel's 70th week is described as a seven-year period marked by:

- A covenant made by a future prince (Dan. 9:27)

- A midpoint betrayal (abomination of desolation)

- Unparalleled desolation and wrath

This aligns with what Jesus calls "the great tribulation" (Matt. 24:15–21) and what John describes in Revelation 6–19. During this time:

- God pours out judgment on a Christ-rejecting world.

- Israel is brought to repentance and national restoration.

- The kingdoms of the world are crushed.

It is not a season for building the Church—it is a time of wrath, purging, and preparation for the kingdom.

I briefly want to address Antioch Epiphanes. Some have thought that this was a fulfillment of the prophecy. So, the question that sometimes comes up is this, "Was the "prince who shall come" in Daniel 9:26–27 Antiochus Epiphanes?

Some interpreters — particularly in historicist or preterist schools of thought — have claimed that the "prince who shall come" refers to Antiochus IV Epiphanes, the Seleucid king who desecrated the temple around 167 B.C. during the intertestamental period. He notoriously sacrificed a pig on the altar and erected a statue of Zeus in the Holy of Holies, sparking the Maccabean revolt.

There's no doubt Antiochus Epiphanes is a foreshadowing or type of the coming Antichrist. Even Daniel 8 gives a vision of him. But to interpret Daniel 9:26–27 as fulfilled entirely by him fails on several important grounds — both historical and contextual.

1. The Timeline Doesn't Fit

Daniel 9:25-27 lays out a precise 490-year prophetic timeline, including:

- 69 weeks (483 years) from the decree to rebuild Jerusalem to the arrival of the Messiah.

- A "cutting off" of the Messiah (fulfilled in Christ's crucifixion)

- A final 70th week of desolation and covenant-breaking

Antiochus lived and ruled before the Messiah ever came — around 175–164 B.C., roughly 200 years prior to the crucifixion. That means he cannot fulfill the "prince who shall come" in a chronological sequence that explicitly occurs after the Messiah is cut off.

2. The Destruction of Jerusalem Occurs After the Messiah Is Cut Off

Daniel 9:26 states:

"...after the sixty-two weeks, Messiah shall be cut off, but not for Himself. And the people of the prince who shall come shall destroy the city and the sanctuary..."

This points forward to the destruction of Jerusalem and the Temple in A.D. 70 by the Romans — not back to Antiochus' desecration in the 2nd century B.C.

That "prince who shall come" is not from Antiochus' Seleucid Greek empire, but from the people who destroyed the sanctuary — the Romans. That's a direct reference to the future Roman origin or affiliation of the final Antichrist.

3. Jesus Treated It as Future

Jesus referred to Daniel's prophecy of the "abomination of desolation" in Matthew 24:15, saying:

> *"So, when you see standing in the holy place 'the abomination that causes desolation,' spoken of through the prophet Daniel — let the reader understand…"*

Jesus taught this was still future, even though Antiochus' abomination had occurred over 150 years earlier.

If Antiochus was the full and final fulfillment of Daniel 9:27, then Jesus — speaking in 30 A.D. — would not have referred to it as something yet to come.

4. Antiochus Was a Type — Not the Fulfillment

Antiochus Epiphanes is clearly a type of the final Antichrist, just as:

• Pharaoh was a type of Satan.

• David was a type of Christ.

- Babylon was a type of the final global system.

Daniel 8 describes a "little horn" (Antiochus) distinct from the "little horn" of Daniel 7 (the final Antichrist). They share characteristics, but they are not the same person.

Types are common in prophetic literature — shadows that point forward to greater realities. Antiochus' desecration prefigured the future abomination that the final Antichrist will commit during the Tribulation (2 Thessalonians 2:4; Revelation 13).

5. Antiochus never made the 7-Year Covenant

Daniel 9:27 states that the prince will confirm a covenant with many for one week (7 years), and in the middle of the week, he will break it and bring about desolation.

There is no record of Antiochus ever making or breaking a 7-year covenant with Israel. But this is exactly what the future Antichrist will do, as affirmed by Jesus (Matthew 24:15) and Paul (2 Thessalonians 2:3-4).

Antiochus Epiphanes is not the "prince who shall come" in Daniel 9:26-27. He is a foreshadowing, but not the fulfillment. The prince described in Daniel 9 is:

- Yet future in the days of Christ

- Associated with the Roman people.

- Involved in a seven-year covenant with Israel.

- Breaks it at the midpoint.

- Brings about the final desolation and is later destroyed.

This matches the character and mission of the final Antichrist, not a Seleucid king.

Why the Church Must Be Absent

Nowhere in Revelation 6–18 is the Church mentioned as being on earth. The Church appears in chapters 2–3 in the form of letters to local churches. But from chapter 4 onward, John is caught up into heaven, and the scene shifts to judgment on earth. From that point:

- The Church is not seen again until Revelation 19, when she returns with Christ, not waiting for Him.

This confirms a vital truth: the Church is with Christ during the Tribulation, not on earth enduring it.

Why?

Been redeemed spiritually.

- Been sealed with the Spirit.

- Been promised not to endure wrath (1 Thess. 5:9)

- Been caught up to meet Christ (1 Thess. 4:17)

Theological Fulfillment: Spiritual First, Then Physical

Here we return to the vital theology we discussed earlier. The first coming of Christ brought spiritual redemption:

- Justification by faith

- The gift of the Holy Spirit

- The creation of the Church

But we remain in mortal, corruptible bodies. As Paul says in Romans 8:23:

"...we ourselves, who have the first fruits of the Spirit, groan inwardly as we wait eagerly for our adoption as sons, the redemption of our bodies."

The second coming of Christ will bring physical redemption:

- The glorification of the saints (1 Cor. 15:51–53)

- The defeat of the Antichrist (2 Thess. 2:8)

- The establishment of a kingdom on earth (Rev. 20:4)

The Rapture, then, is the transition point between these two phases. It is when the spiritually redeemed Church is physically transformed. This must happen before Christ begins His covenant work with Israel again and before He pours out wrath on a world that rejected Him.

The Church's Current Mission: Ambassadors in a Foreign Land

Right now, the Church operates in a fallen world, still under the dominion of Satan (2 Cor. 4:4). We are not called to conquer it—we are called to witness in it.

Paul calls believers "ambassadors for Christ" (2 Cor. 5:20). We represent a heavenly kingdom, and we invite the lost into reconciliation with God. Through prayer, proclamation, and perseverance, we function as God's restraining force—the vessel through which the Spirit holds back evil.

But this mission is temporary. Once the Church is complete—once every member of the Body is brought in—the Bride will be called home. At that moment, the age of grace concludes, and the final week of Daniel's prophecy begins.

God's Pattern: Separation Before Judgment

God is consistent. Before He judges, He removes His people:

- Enoch was taken before the flood (Gen. 5:24)

- Noah entered the ark before judgment fell (Gen. 7:16)

- Lot was removed before fire rained down (Gen. 19:22)

- Rahab was secured before Jericho fell (Josh. 2:21)

In the same pattern, the Church will be removed before the wrath of the Tribulation falls.

What the Tribulation Is Not

Let us be clear: the Tribulation is not a time of evangelistic revival led by the Church.

It is:

- A time of judgment on unbelievers

- A time of refining for Israel

- A time of transition from Satan's rule to Christ's reign

Yes, many will be saved during this time (praise God)— through the ministry of 144,000 sealed Jewish evangelists, through the two witnesses in Jerusalem, and through angelic proclamations (Rev. 14:6–7). But this is not the Church's mission field. The Bride will already be with her Bridegroom.

A Glorious Distinction

The 70th week of Daniel is a Jewish prophecy, meant for Israel and the nations. The Church is a mystery revealed, not subject to this timeline but called to a separate destiny.

The Church:

- Began after the 69th week.

- Ends before the 70th week.

- Is not destined for wrath but glory.

To include the Church in the Tribulation is to collapse the beautiful distinction between God's covenant with Israel and His calling of the Bride of Christ.

Let us therefore hold firm:

- The Church age is an age of spiritual victory.

- The Rapture is the moment of glorification.

- The Tribulation is the return to Israel's final refinement.

- The Second Coming is the moment of physical conquest.

We live now as ambassadors. But soon, we will be called citizens. Then heirs. Then kings and priests. All of it began with Daniel, kneeling in prayer, receiving a vision of what would come—and what would not belong to the Church.

Chapter 6

The Day of the Lord vs. The Day of Christ

"For you yourselves are fully aware that the day of the Lord will come like a thief in the night... While people are saying, 'There is peace and security,' then sudden destruction will come upon them... But you are not in darkness, brothers, for that day to surprise you like a thief... For God has not destined us for wrath, but to obtain salvation through our Lord Jesus Christ."

— 1 Thessalonians 5:2-9

Few distinctions in biblical eschatology have caused more confusion than the phrases "the Day of the Lord" and "the Day of Christ." Though they sound similar, they refer to profoundly different moments in God's redemptive timeline. To collapse them into one is to risk misunderstanding the timing of the Rapture, the nature of God's wrath, and the hope that the Church clings to in the last days.

Both phrases speak of divine intervention. Both speak of a time when God acts decisively in human history. But where one points to judgment, the other announces joy. Where one evokes terror for the wicked, the other evokes comfort for the believer. The distinction is not merely academic — it is theological, practical, and essential.

The Day of the Lord: Judgment on a Rebellious World

The Day of the Lord is a phrase that echoes throughout the Old

Testament prophets. Isaiah, Joel, Amos, and Zephaniah, among others, all warned of this day. It is described as a time of darkness and not light, of vengeance and not mercy. It is the moment when God arises from His dwelling place to shake the earth and bring justice to a rebellious world.

Isaiah cries out, *"Wail, for the day of the Lord is near; as destruction from the Almighty it will come"* (Isaiah 13:6). Joel declares, *"The day of the Lord is great and very terrible; who can endure it?"* (Joel 2:11). Zephaniah warns, *"The great day of the Lord is near... That day is a day of wrath, a day of distress and anguish..."* (Zephaniah 1:14–15).

These passages paint a vivid and sobering picture. The Day of the Lord is not a singular event but a season of divine wrath — a time when the restraint of God is lifted, and His judgment is poured out on the nations. It includes, but is not limited to, the Tribulation period and culminates in the return of Christ to destroy the Antichrist and establish His kingdom on earth.

Paul echoes this understanding in 1 Thessalonians 5:2-3, where he writes, *"The day of the Lord will come like a thief in the night. While people are saying, 'Peace and safety,' destruction will come on them suddenly... and they will not escape."* Here, the Day of the Lord is sudden, terrifying, and inescapable for the world.

Notably, Paul uses third-person language — "they," not "we." This is critical. The Church, he says, is not in darkness that this day should overtake them. They are not appointed to wrath (1 Thess. 5:9). Why?

Because they are awaiting a different day — the Day of Christ.

The Day of Christ: Redemption for the Bride

The phrase "Day of Christ" appears primarily in Paul's letters, and it conveys an entirely different tone. It is not a day of vengeance but a day of completion. It is not wrath but reward. It is the day when the Church, the Bride of Christ, is gathered to her Lord and ushered into glory.

Paul refers to this day in Philippians 1:6, "...He who began a good work in you will bring it to completion at the day of Jesus Christ." Again, in verse 10, he prays that believers may be pure and blameless for the day of Christ. In Philippians 2:16, he expresses hope that he may rejoice on that day, having not labored in vain.

These references are intimate, joyful, and personal. The Day of Christ is a day of evaluation and reward, not destruction. It includes the Bema Seat judgment (2 Corinthians 5:10), where believers are rewarded for their service, and the marriage supper of the Lamb, where the Church enters into full fellowship with Christ.

This day begins with the Rapture — the catching away of the Church to meet Christ in the air. It is the day when faith becomes sight, when the mortal puts on immortality, when the groaning of creation gives way to the glory of redemption.

Contrasting the Two Days

To fully appreciate the distinction, consider the characteristics of each:

The Day of the Lord is often associated with wrath, judgment, darkness, and terror. It is directed at the rebellious world and apostate Israel. It comes unexpectedly upon the unbelieving. Its tone is one of alarm. It is God dealing with the world in justice.

The Day of Christ, however, is linked to hope, reward, and joy. It is directed at the Church. It is anticipated eagerly. It is the day when the Bridegroom comes for His Bride. It is God dealing with the Church in grace and fulfillment.

While both days are in the eschatological future, they do not occur at the same time. The Day of Christ precedes the Day of the Lord. The Church is caught up, glorified, and rewarded before God begins His wrath upon the earth.

Paul makes this clear in 2 Thessalonians 2. Some in the church at Thessalonica feared that the Day of the Lord had already come. Paul reassures them that it has not — and cannot — unless the departure happens first.

Many translations of 2 Thessalonians 2:3 render the Greek word *apostasia* as "rebellion" or "apostasy," but it can also be interpreted as "departure." The verse is commonly interpreted to mean that a spiritual falling away must occur before the Antichrist is revealed.

However, there is a compelling case—linguistically, historically, and contextually—that *apostasia* in this passage may instead refer to a physical departure: specifically, the Rapture of the Church.

The Greek word used here, *apostasia*, is derived from the verb aphistēmi, as seen in 2 Timothy 4:6, which means "to depart," "to remove," or "to withdraw." It can describe both physical and metaphorical departures, including rebellion, defection, or similar actions. While *apostasia* eventually became associated with doctrinal apostasy in later theological language, its original and broader meaning simply implies a departure from a place or position. Importantly, this noun appears only twice in the New Testament—here in 2 Thessalonians 2:3, and in Acts 21:21, where it refers to Jews "forsaking" the law of Moses, but not necessarily in an end-times doctrinal context.

Early English Bible translations reflect this broader meaning. In fact, before the King James Version of 1611, many translators rendered **apostasia** as "departure", not "rebellion." The Tyndale Bible (1534), the Cranmer Bible (1539), the Geneva Bible (1560), and even the Beza Latin translation all used a term equivalent to **"departure"** in English or Latin (*discessio*). These translators were not inventing new doctrine; they were rendering the Greek text according to its literal sense, without the doctrinal biases that influenced later eschatological interpretations.

Support for this reading is also found among Greek scholars and theologians. Dr. Kenneth Wuest, a noted Greek scholar, argues that the word refers to a spatial or physical departure. E. Schuyler English, in *Re-thinking the Rapture*, affirms the same view, and a number of Pre-Tribulational teachers—including J. Dwight Pentecost, John Walvoord, and others—have acknowledged that this interpretation fits the context of Paul's argument.

This interpretation is especially coherent when you consider the immediate context of the passage. Paul begins the chapter by referring to *"the coming of our Lord Jesus Christ and our being gathered together to Him"* (2 Thess. 2:1), which clearly speaks of the Rapture. He then reassures the Thessalonians that "that day"—the Day of the Lord—will not come unless the *apostasia* occurs first. Suppose apostasia means the physical departure of the Church. In that case, the sequence is logical: first the Rapture, then the revealing of the man of sin, then the outpouring of divine judgment.

Even if one chooses not to dogmatically assert that *apostasia* must mean the Rapture in this context, it must still be admitted that the word itself does not inherently mean spiritual rebellion. That is an interpretive choice. The Pre-Tribulational understanding—that the departure refers to the physical removal of the Church—is not only linguistically viable, but also harmonizes well with Paul's theology and with the sequence of end-times events he outlines.

In light of the grammar, historical translations, and theological consistency, interpreting *apostasia* in 2 Thessalonians 2:3 as the Rapture is not a novel theory. It is a historically grounded, textually supported, and doctrinally consistent view that affirms the hope that believers will be "caught up" before the judgments of the Day of the Lord begin.

Paul goes on to say that the restrainer must first be removed. (2 Thessalonians 2:6). As we've seen, the Church, indwelt by the Holy Spirit, is the restraining force in the world today. Once the Church is taken out of the way, the full mystery of lawlessness is unleashed. The Antichrist rises. The Day of the Lord begins.

Spiritual Victory Before Physical Judgment

This order is not accidental. It reflects the structure of redemptive history. The Church is the fruit of Christ's first coming — the spiritual victory over sin and death. The Tribulation is the prelude to His second coming — the physical victory over the kingdoms of this world.

To place the Church within the Day of the Lord is to reverse this order. It is to blur the lines between reward and wrath, between joy and judgment. It is to suggest that Christ's Bride must endure the very wrath from which she was already delivered.

"This mortal must put on immortality." This is our hope, our inheritance. We are not waiting for wrath. We are waiting for a wedding. We are not preparing for war. We are preparing for glory.

Anchoring Our Hope

Understanding this distinction matters because it anchors our hope.

The early Church comforted one another with the promise of the Rapture. They did not brace themselves for global judgment; they looked up to the Savior. Paul exhorted them to "encourage one another with these words" (1 Thess. 4:18).

So should we.

We live in a world that trembles on the brink. The shadows are lengthening. The deception is growing. But we do not despair. For us, the trumpet is not a call to battle — it is a call to home.

The Day of the Lord may be dark, but the Day of Christ is dawning, and we are not of the night, but of the day.

Chapter 7

Caught Up Before Wrath: Not Appointed Unto Judgment

"For God has not destined us for wrath, but to obtain salvation through our Lord Jesus Christ."

— 1 Thessalonians 5:9

"Much more then, being now justified by his blood, we shall be saved from wrath through him."

— Romans 5:9

If the Church is to go through the Tribulation (even if the church is protected), then the very nature of salvation, the function of justification, and the promise of peace with God must all be reconsidered. But Scripture is clear: the believer, having been justified by faith, is not appointed unto wrath. There is no ambiguity in Paul's words to the Thessalonians or the Romans.

The believer is not preserved through wrath. He is saved from it.

This chapter focuses on one of the most overlooked but vital theological pillars in support of the Pre-Tribulational Rapture — the doctrine that the Church, as the blood-bought Bride of Christ, is removed before God's judgment is poured out upon the earth.

The Nature of Wrath

There is a categorical difference between the trials of life in a fallen world and the wrath of God. Believers today face persecution, hardship, and suffering — but these are not the wrath of God. Tribulation in this life is the result of a fallen world, the opposition of the enemy, and the cost of discipleship. Jesus promised that in this world, we would have trouble (John 16:33). But He also promised peace in Him.

The Tribulation, however — the 70th week of Daniel — is not merely trouble. It is divine wrath. The culmination of the ages. The seals, trumpets, and bowls in Revelation are not expressions of Satanic fury alone; they are the outpouring of God's righteous judgment upon a rebellious world (Rev. 6:16- 17). The earth's inhabitants cry out not because of war or famine alone, but because "the great day of [God's] wrath has come." The Church, by its very nature, cannot be present for that outpouring, because the wrath of God was already satisfied in Christ.

Salvation and Separation

When Jesus bore the sin of the world on the cross, He also bore its wrath. "He was crushed for our iniquities... and the punishment that brought us peace was upon Him" (Isaiah 53:5). To say that the Church must endure divine wrath is to say that the blood of Christ was insufficient to satisfy the justice of God fully.

This is not merely a question of timing. It is a question of atonement. Romans 5:9 settles it clearly: "Since we have now been justified by His blood, how much more shall we be saved from wrath through Him?" The believer, having been reconciled to God, cannot face judgment from the same God who now declares him righteous. There is no double jeopardy in the kingdom of God.

A People Set Apart

The pattern of divine deliverance is deeply embedded in Scripture. As stated previously, Noah was saved before the flood.

Lot was removed before the fire. Israel was spared from the judgment of Egypt through the blood of the lamb. Rahab was secured before Jericho fell.

God's people have always been distinguished from the objects of His wrath. And in the New Testament, the Church is called a peculiar people, a royal priesthood, not of the world, set apart for glory, not destruction.

Typology: Sons of the Flesh vs. Sons of Promise

Biblical typology reinforces this separation. In the pages of Scripture, God unveils truth through recurring patterns — types and shadows that prefigure deeper realities. One of the most profound of these is the theme of firstborn by the flesh versus second-born by promise.

Abraham had two sons: Ishmael and Isaac. Ishmael was born of the flesh — a product of human effort and impatience. Isaac was born by promise — a miracle, made possible by divine intervention after all human strength was exhausted. Though Ishmael came first, he was not the heir. God said clearly: "In Isaac your seed shall be called" (Genesis 21:12).

Paul seizes on this in Galatians 4, explaining that Ishmael represents the old covenant, born at Sinai, and Isaac represents the new, born from above. Isaac is a picture of the Church — supernaturally born by grace through faith, not law or lineage.

The same pattern emerges with Esau and Jacob. Esau was firstborn, the natural heir. But Jacob, the younger, grasped the heel and received the promise. "Jacob, I loved, but Esau I hated," says the Lord (Romans 9:13). Again, the pattern is unmistakable: the firstborn of the flesh is set aside for the second-born of promise.

This is not just poetic repetition. It is a doctrinally rich typology.

Israel is the natural seed — the firstborn of the covenant. The Church is the spiritual seed — the supernatural Body born from above. The two are distinct. Their identities, callings, and destinies differ. Israel will one day inherit her promised kingdom on earth. The Church will be caught up to inherit glory with her heavenly Bridegroom.

To place the Church in the Tribulation — the time of Jacob's trouble — is to confuse Isaac with Ishmael, Jacob with Esau, grace with law, promise with flesh.

God's Restraint Through His People

We must also revisit the restrainer in 2 Thessalonians 2. Paul speaks of a force currently holding back the revelation of the man of lawlessness. This restraint must be removed before the Antichrist is revealed and the Day of the Lord unfolds.

Many scholars and pastors throughout Church history have identified the restrainer as the Holy Spirit working through the Church. The Church — indwelt by the Spirit — is the salt of the earth, the light of the world, and a restraining presence against lawlessness. When the Church is removed, the restraining influence is lifted. The world is handed over to delusion, deception, and destruction.

This, again, shows that the Church must be removed before the judgments of the Day of the Lord. The Bride is caught up before the Beast rises up.

Wrath and Reward Do Not Mix

Finally, consider the consistent contrast between the tone of judgment passages and those speaking to the Church.

Revelation 6–18 is full of horror, plagues, curses, and death. But Paul's letters speak of joy, hope, expectation, reward, and reunion. We are not told to watch for destruction but to wait for our Savior from heaven (Philippians 3:20). We are not told to endure wrath but to look for the blessed hope and the glorious appearing of our great God and Savior (Titus 2:13).

The tone is entirely different — because the destinies are different.

The Rapture is not an escape plan. It is the next chapter in a redemptive story where the blood of the Lamb has already secured our salvation — body, soul, and spirit. The wrath of God will come upon a world that rejected the Son. But the Bride will not be beaten before the wedding. She will be caught up, transformed, glorified — and then judgment will fall.

This is not wishful thinking. It is biblical consistency. It is theological integrity. And it is the unshakable hope of every believer who longs for His appearing.

Chapter 8

The Voice Like a Trumpet: *Harpazō* and the Pattern of Sudden Removal

"For the Lord himself will descend from heaven with a cry of command, with the voice of an archangel, and with the trumpet of God. And the dead in Christ will rise first. Then we who are alive, who are left, will be caught up [harpazō] together with them in the clouds to meet the Lord in the air, and so we will always be with the Lord."

— 1 Thessalonians 4:16-17

"Behold! I tell you a mystery. We shall not all sleep, but we shall all be changed... in a moment, in the twinkling of an eye, at the last trumpet."

— 1 Corinthians 15:51-52

The event known as the Rapture is not a theological abstraction or hopeful metaphor. It is a sudden, supernatural, physical event that Scripture describes with extraordinary clarity and urgency. At its center is a single Greek word—*harpazō*—translated in English as "caught up." This word, found in 1 Thessalonians 4:17, captures the essence of what will happen to believers at the return of Christ for His Church: they will be seized, snatched away, removed in a flash from this world to meet the Lord in the air.

In this chapter, we will examine the meaning and force of *harpazō*, the prophetic use of trumpets, and the consistent biblical pattern of sudden removals prior to divine judgment.

Together, these elements confirm the nature and necessity of the Rapture as a distinct, imminent event within God's redemptive timeline.

Harpazō: The Snatching Away

The Greek word harpazō is a powerful and violent verb. It means to seize, snatch, or carry off suddenly. It appears fourteen times in the New Testament and is used in contexts that emphasize force, speed, and divine intervention.

- In Acts 8:39, the Spirit of the Lord "caught up" Philip and transported him to another location.

- In 2 Corinthians 12:2–4, Paul describes being "caught up" into the third heaven—into paradise itself.

- In Revelation 12:5, the male child (Christ) is "caught up" to God and His throne.

In each case, *harpazō* describes a supernatural removal from one place to another, often to preserve, protect, or glorify. When Paul uses this word in 1 Thessalonians 4:17 to describe what will happen to living believers at Christ's coming, he is not inventing a poetic metaphor. He is describing a divine act of sudden evacuation.

The Latin translation of *harpazō* is rapturo, from which we get the

English word "Rapture." Though critics often point out that the word "Rapture" does not appear in English Bibles, the concept is deeply embedded in the biblical text. *Harpazō* is the original, inspired word— and it means exactly what believers throughout history have understood: a sudden catching away.

The Trumpet of God

Paul connects the Rapture to the sounding of a trumpet— a theme rooted deeply in both Testaments. In 1 Corinthians 15:52, he writes, "in a moment, in the twinkling of an eye, at the last trumpet… we shall be changed." Likewise, in 1 Thessalonians 4:16, "the trumpet of God" accompanies the Lord's descent.

Trumpets in Scripture are used to:

1. Announce divine visitation (Exodus 19:16–19)

2. Gather the assembly (Numbers 10:1–4)

3. Signal war or judgment (Joel 2:1)

4. Mark the coronation of a king (1 Kings 1:34)

5. Celebrate deliverance (Leviticus 25:9)

At the Rapture, all these meanings converge. The trumpet signals Christ's arrival, gathers His saints, proclaims the final victory over death, and inaugurates the Bride's ascent to her heavenly home. It is not a trumpet of alarm—it is a trumpet of redemption. I would also add that it is a notification. The enemy of God has just been put on notice that after all of this time, his time, is at hand.

Importantly, this "last trumpet" must be distinguished from the trumpet judgments in Revelation, which are instruments of wrath upon the earth. The trumpet of 1 Corinthians 15 and 1 Thessalonians 4 is sounded for the Church—not in judgment, but in rescue. It is a call upward, not an alarm downward.

Patterns of Removal Before Judgment

Throughout the Bible, God consistently removes His righteous people before unleashing judgment on the wicked. This pattern is not coincidental—it reveals God's character and His commitment to distinguish the righteous from the unrighteous. As we have discussed,

- **Noah** was preserved in the ark before the floodwaters rose (Genesis 6–7).

- **Lot** was removed from Sodom before fire fell from heaven (Genesis 19).

- **Enoch** walked with God and "was not, for God took him" (Genesis 5:24)—a clear picture of pre-judgment removal.

- **Rahab** and her family were safely marked before Jericho's fall (Joshua 2, 6).

- **Israel** was protected in Goshen while Egypt suffered plague after plague (Exodus 8:22; 9:26).

- **The male child** in Revelation 12 is caught up to God before the dragon can devour him—a symbol of Christ, but also a picture of divine protection by removal.

Each of these examples points to a God who rescues before He judges. The Rapture is not a disruption in God's plan.

It is the next in a long line of divine interventions where the righteous are removed and the wicked are judged.

The Immediacy and Comfort of Harpazō

Paul urges the Thessalonian believers to "encourage one another with these words" (1 Thess. 4:18). He does not present the Rapture as something to endure, but as something to hope for. There is no call to brace for divine wrath—only to look up and be ready.

This is the tone of imminency. The Rapture could happen at any moment. There are no required signs or precursors. It is an unexpected, supernatural event that will occur "in the twinkling of an eye." This is why Jesus and the apostles repeatedly call the Church to watchfulness, readiness, and expectancy.

Jesus said, "I go to prepare a place for you... I will come again and will take you to myself" (John 14:3). The Rapture is the fulfillment of that promise—the personal return of Christ to gather His Bride. It is not a vague spiritual moment, but a real and physical transformation, when "this mortal must put on immortality."

The voice like a trumpet will call. The heavens will open. And in a moment, those who are in Christ will rise—caught up, not left behind; glorified, not judged. This is the blessed hope, the harbinger of the resurrection, the comfort of the Church in a world trembling on the edge of wrath. The Bridegroom is coming. The invitation is open. The trumpet will sound.

Chapter 9

The Jewish Wedding and the Church's Blessed Hope

"In My Father's house are many rooms… I go to prepare a place for you. And if I go… I will come again and will take you to Myself, that where I am you may be also."

— John 14:2–3

"Let us rejoice and exult and give him the glory, for the marriage of the Lamb has come, and his Bride has made herself ready…"

— Revelation 19:7

The Rapture is not merely an escape from wrath — it is a divine appointment with the Bridegroom. To truly appreciate the beauty of this upcoming event, we must understand the ancient Jewish wedding model — a tradition rich in prophetic symbolism. Jesus' words in the Upper Room, Paul's references to the Bride, and John's apocalyptic vision in Revelation all draw upon this rich cultural and spiritual background.

In this chapter, we explore how the structure of a first- century Jewish wedding reveals the relational and redemptive dimensions of the Rapture. The imagery is not incidental. It is intentional — a divine pattern embedded in covenant tradition to unveil the mystery of the Church's destiny.

The Betrothal: Covenant and Commitment

In the Jewish custom, the marriage process began not with a proposal, but with a betrothal — a binding covenant agreement between the bridegroom and the bride. It was formal, legal, and sealed with a bride price — the mohar — paid by the groom to purchase the right to marry her.

The Church, too, has been bought with a price — not of silver or gold, but with the precious blood of Christ (1 Corinthians 6:20). Our betrothal to Christ is secure. Paul writes, "I betrothed you to one husband, to present you as a pure virgin to Christ" (2 Corinthians 11:2). This is more than metaphor. It is covenantal reality.

Once betrothed, the bride was legally considered set apart for her husband. Though they had not yet consummated the marriage, she was his — and he hers.

The Groom Departs to Prepare a Place

After the covenant was sealed, the groom would leave his bride and return to his father's house. There, he would begin to build a bridal chamber — an addition to his father's estate, carefully constructed and prepared as the new home for the bride.

This is precisely the imagery Jesus used in John 14:2–3 when He said,

"I go to prepare a place for you... and I will come again." Jesus, our Bridegroom, has returned to the Father's house — not to delay, but to prepare. And just like the ancient groom, He will return when the place is ready.

Importantly, the exact timing of the groom's return was not set by the groom himself. It was determined by the father. Only when the father declared the bridal chamber complete could the groom go and claim his bride. This echoes Jesus' words in Matthew 24:36 — "No one knows the day or hour... but the Father only."

The Bride Waits in Readiness

During this period of separation, the bride was to remain pure, prepared, and watchful. She did not know the day of his return, but she knew it would come. She was to remain vigilant — her lamp trimmed, her garments ready.

This is the consistent charge given to the Church throughout the New Testament. "Stay awake," Jesus said. "Be ready, for the Son of Man is coming at an hour you do not expect" (Matthew 24:42-44). Paul exhorted the Thessalonians to be "children of the light" — not asleep, but alert (1 Thess. 5:6).

The Rapture is not only the next event on the prophetic calendar — it is the next moment in the love story between Christ and His Bride.

The Midnight Shout and the Gathering

When the father gave permission, the groom would gather his friends and go to the bride's village. As they approached, they would sound a trumpet **or** shout aloud — a cry that pierced the night and woke the sleeping town. This was the long-awaited moment. The bride, often awakened from sleep, would rise, gather her things, and be taken — sometimes lifted up and carried — to meet the groom and join him in the procession.

This mirrors Paul's vivid picture in 1 Thessalonians 4:16- 17 — the Lord descending with a shout, the trumpet of God sounding, and the saints being caught up to meet Him in the air.

The bride did not return to her old house. She was taken to the home the groom had prepared. The Rapture, likewise, is a heavenward movement, not a return of Christ to the earth. It is a personal reunion, not a political conquest.

The Seven-Day Wedding and Revelation's Timeline

After the bride was taken, the couple would enter the bridal chamber for seven days, while the guests celebrated. Only after this period would the couple emerge publicly and begin life together.

This aligns prophetically with the Church's removal before the seven-year Tribulation. While the world faces judgment, the Bride is in the Father's house — safe, secure, and celebrating the marriage supper of the Lamb (Revelation 19:7-9).

After the seven years, Christ returns to the earth — not for His Bride, but with His Bride — to establish His kingdom.

The Bride Is Not Appointed to Wrath

It would be unthinkable for a bridegroom to batter his bride before their wedding. Likewise, the Church — purified by grace, secured by covenant, and set apart for glory — is not subject to the judgments that fall upon the earth. As Paul said plainly, "God has not destined us for wrath, but to obtain salvation through our Lord Jesus Christ" (1 Thessalonians 5:9).

The Jewish wedding model is not just a beautiful tradition. It is prophetic architecture. Every detail — from the covenant, to the preparation, to the trumpet, to the consummation — aligns with the biblical teaching of the Rapture and the Church's role as the Bride of Christ.

The Rapture is not an interruption. It is an invitation — to intimacy, to glory, to a kingdom not made with hands. We are not waiting for a warlord to crush the nations. We are waiting for a Bridegroom to sweep us into the chambers of joy. The trumpet will sound, the shout will ring, and the Bride will rise. And we shall be with Him — forever.

Chapter 10

The Separation of the Sheep and the Bride

"When the Son of Man comes in His glory, and all the angels with Him, then He will sit on His glorious throne. Before Him will be gathered all the nations, and He will separate people one from another as a shepherd separates the sheep from the goats."

— Matthew 25:31–32

"And to her it was granted to be arrayed in fine linen, clean and bright, for the fine linen is the righteous acts of the saints... Blessed are those who are invited to the marriage supper of the Lamb."

— Revelation 19:8–9

The parable of the sheep and goats, found in Matthew 25:31-46, is often confused with the Rapture. At first glance, both involve a gathering. Both involve a coming of Christ. But a closer, more careful reading reveals that these are two entirely different events, separated by time, purpose, and audience. The Bride is not the sheep. And the sheep are not the Bride.

Understanding this distinction helps clarify the prophetic timeline and confirms the Pre-Tribulational view of the Rapture— not just as a rescue, but as a relational reunion with Christ, **before** the final judgment of the nations.

Two Very Different Scenes

In 1 Thessalonians 4 and 1 Corinthians 15, Paul describes the Rapture as a sudden event where believers are caught up to meet Christ "in the air." No mention is made of judgment. The tone is hopeful, triumphant, and exclusive to believers. The emphasis is on resurrection, reunion, and transformation.

By contrast, in Matthew 25, Jesus describes a very different event:

- He comes not in the air, but to earth, seated on a throne of judgment.

- He is accompanied by angels, and all the nations are gathered before Him.

- The purpose is not reunion, but separation — sorting the righteous (sheep) from the unrighteous (goats).

- The result is not glorification, but entrance into or exclusion from the Millennial Kingdom.

This is not the catching up of the Bride. This is the judgment of the nations, based on how they treated Christ's "brothers" — likely referring to Israel and perhaps believing Jews during the Tribulation.

The Timing: Post-Tribulation Judgment

The timing of Matthew 25 is clear: "When the Son of Man comes in His glory… then He will sit on His glorious throne" (v. 31). This scene happens after the return of Christ in Revelation 19, after the battle of

Armageddon, and after the fall of Babylon. The Tribulation has ended. The Beast has been defeated. Now comes the moment to determine who among the survivors of the nations will enter the Millennial Kingdom.

This is a judgment of the living, not the dead. There is no resurrection here — only those who have lived through the Tribulation and now stand before the King. The wicked are cast into "eternal punishment," and the righteous inherit the kingdom.

Again, this is nothing like the Rapture, where believers are glorified and taken to the Father's house. Here, people are judged on the basis of their deeds — particularly how they responded to God's people during the most trying time in human history.

The Bride Has Already Been Taken

The Bride of Christ — the Church — is not present in the sheep and goats judgment as a group to be judged. She is already with Christ. She was caught up before the Tribulation, celebrated the marriage supper of the Lamb, and now returns with Him as Revelation 19 shows:

"The armies of heaven, arrayed in fine linen, white and pure, were following Him on white horses."

-(Rev. 19:14)

That "fine linen" is the same clothing described in verse 8— the righteous acts of the saints. The Church is not being sorted at this point. She has already been glorified.

Instead, she stands beside Christ as co-heir and co-regent. Paul reminds us in 1 Corinthians 6:2, "Do you not know that the saints will judge the world?" The Church participates in judgment — she is not the object of it.

The Identity of the Sheep

The "sheep" in Matthew 25 are not the Church. They are those from the nations who, during the Tribulation, showed kindness to Christ's "brothers" — likely referring to faithful Jewish believers, the 144,000, or Tribulation saints. These sheep are Gentile survivors of the Tribulation who did not take the mark of the Beast, did not bow to the Antichrist, and showed mercy and loyalty to the suffering people of God.

They are welcomed into the Kingdom on earth — not into the heavenly New Jerusalem. They are not glorified. They are not raptured. They remain in human bodies to populate the Millennial Kingdom, where Christ will rule from Jerusalem.

The Church Is Not Appointed to This Judgment

This judgment is one of **works**, not grace. The sheep are judged "according to what they have done." But the Church, according to Romans 8:1, is already justified: "There is therefore now no condemnation for those who are in Christ Jesus." Our judgment took place at the cross, and our reward is received at the Bema Seat (2 Cor. 5:10), a separate event that happens in heaven, not on earth.

To conflate the sheep with the Church is to confuse the entire structure of end-times prophecy. The Bride is taken before wrath. The sheep are evaluated after wrath. The Church is glorified. The sheep are preserved. One is a covenantal union. The other is a millennial invitation.

The Bride will not be sorted like livestock. She has already been chosen, adorned, and welcomed into the chambers of the King. The Rapture is her gathering. The judgment of the nations is something else entirely. The sheep inherit the earth — but the Bride inherits the heavens.

Chapter 11

The Trumpet Confusion: Distinguishing God's Trumpet from the Seventh

"In a moment, in the twinkling of an eye, at the last trumpet. For the trumpet will sound, and the dead will be raised imperishable, and we shall be changed."

— 1 Corinthians 15:52

"Then the seventh angel blew his trumpet, and there were loud voices in heaven, saying, 'The kingdom of the world has become the kingdom of our Lord and of His Christ...'"

— Revelation 11:15

One of the most debated interpretive issues in eschatology is Paul's reference to the "last trumpet" in 1 Corinthians 15 and its relation—or lack thereof—to the seventh trumpet in the book of Revelation. We spoke of this previously in brief. Some claim these must refer to the same event. If so, the Rapture would occur at or near the midpoint or end of the Tribulation, after the trumpet judgments unfold. But the text does not require this conflation, and in fact, undermines both the chronological flow and the distinct purposes of these two trumpets.

To understand the Rapture biblically, we must ask: What does Paul mean by "last trumpet"? Is it the final trumpet ever blown in Scripture? Or is it the final trumpet of a distinct series—one that relates to the Church, not to judgment?

The Trumpet in Pauline Theology

In 1 Corinthians 15:52, Paul writes that believers will be changed "in a moment, in the twinkling of an eye, at the last trumpet." This is a parallel passage to 1 Thessalonians 4:16, where "the trumpet of God" accompanies the Lord's descent and the catching up of the saints.

These two passages are clearly connected. Both describe:

- The resurrection of the dead in Christ

- The transformation of the living

- A trumpet sounding

- A sudden, glorifying event

What is notably absent from both is any context of judgment. These trumpets do not summon wrath—they announce reunion. They are a call for the Bride, not a curse upon the world.

In Paul's context, the "last trumpet" is the final trumpet blast for the Church—not the final trumpet in all of human history. The Jewish people were familiar with trumpet calls used to summon, assemble, begin festivals, or announce a journey (Numbers 10:1-10). The "last trumpet" was the final of such calls in a given sequence.

The Trumpets of Revelation

Now contrast that with the trumpet judgments in Revelation 8–11. These are angelic trumpets, not divine or priestly ones. They do not summon the Church. They unleash judgments upon the earth:

1. Hail and fire burn a third of the earth.

2. A mountain-like object turns the sea to blood.

3. A star named Wormwood poisons waters.

4. The sun and moon are struck.

5. Demonic locusts torment men.

6. Four angels slay a third of mankind.

7. The declaration of kingdom transfer (Rev. 11:15) introduces the final bowl judgments.

Each trumpet increases in intensity. They are not encouraging or comforting. They are terrifying. And they belong to a series of sevens: seven seals, seven trumpets, and seven bowls.

To equate Paul's "last trumpet" with the seventh trumpet of Revelation is to collapse two very different systems. Paul was writing decades before John's vision at Patmos. We must take this into account and view it from their perspective, not from ours. His readers would not have been aware of the seven trumpet judgments. They would, however, understand trumpet calls in the context of Jewish feasts, military summons, or wedding customs—all of which Paul draws on elsewhere.

Trumpets in Jewish Typology

The Jewish feast of Rosh Hashanah, known as the Feast of Trumpets, involved multiple trumpet blasts. The last one— Tekiah Gedolah— was the final, long blast that ended the feast. Many scholars believe Paul may be alluding to this final, climactic trumpet as symbolic of the Rapture. It was a joyful sound, not a call to destruction.

The last trumpet for the Church is God's trumpet, not an angel's. It is a trumpet of redemption, not of wrath. It belongs to a heavenly Groom calling for His Bride—not an avenging King judging the earth.

Why the Distinction Matters

If we confuse these trumpets, we distort the timeline. If the "last trumpet" is the seventh trumpet, then the Church must go through at least three-quarters of the Tribulation, enduring horrific judgments that Revelation says are for "those who dwell on the earth"—a phrase never used for the Church. Even if we would say that they are divinely protected from the effects of such judgments, witnessing them, they are still in the midst of them. We will talk about this more in the next chapter.

But Paul reassures us in 1 Thessalonians 1:10 that Jesus "delivers us from the wrath to come." The "last trumpet" signals the end of the Church Age, not the end of the world.

The seventh trumpet in Revelation opens the final stage of wrath. The last trumpet in Paul's letters opens the door to the wedding supper of the Lamb. One summons judgment. The other summons joy.

When the trumpet sounds for the Church, it will not bring fire or plague. It will bring transformation. The dead will rise.

The living will be changed. The Bride will meet her Groom in the air. And the judgment trumpets that follow will not be heard by those who were caught up at the call of grace.

Chapter 12

What Jesus Said: The Olivet Discourse
and the Rapture Debate

"Then two men will be in the field; one will be taken and one left. Two women will be grinding at the mill; one will be taken and one left. Therefore, stay awake, for you do not know on what day your Lord is coming."

— Matthew 24:40-42

"Let not your hearts be troubled... I go to prepare a place for you... I will come again and take you to Myself, that where I am you may be also."

— John 14:1–3

When Jesus sat with His disciples on the Mount of Olives, looking over the temple complex in Jerusalem, they asked Him a pointed question: *"What will be the sign of your coming and of the end of the age?"* (Matthew 24:3). His answer, recorded in what we now call the Olivet Discourse (Matthew 24– 25; Mark 13; Luke 21), is one of the most detailed prophetic messages in all of Scripture.

However, it has also become one of the most debated topics. Does Jesus describe the Rapture in Matthew 24? Or is He referring only to His Second Coming? Does He speak to the Church, or to Israel? The answers to these questions form a hinge upon which much of eschatology turns.

Israel at the Center

To understand the Olivet Discourse, we must begin with its audience and setting. Jesus was speaking to Jewish disciples, outside the Church Age, in the context of the temple, the nation of Israel, and the prophetic timeline of Daniel.

He was not answering a Church-age question. He was answering a question rooted in Israel's expectation of the Messianic Kingdom. Much of what Jesus said—false messiahs, wars, famines, abomination of desolation, fleeing from Judea— are distinctly Jewish in focus. These are the elements of the 70th week of Daniel (Daniel 9:27), the seven-year period commonly referred to as the Tribulation.

The Church, although hidden in mystery during Jesus' ministry (cf. Eph. 3:3–5), is absent from the text until it is implied later.

One Taken, One Left?

The oft-quoted passage from Matthew 24:40-41—"one will be taken, and one left"—has been popularly cited as a reference to the Rapture. But in context, this is not a rescue, but a removal in judgment. Just as in Noah's day "they were unaware until the flood came and swept them all away, so will be the coming of the Son of Man" (v. 39).

Here, the ones "taken" are taken in judgment, not caught up in glory. The setting is not a wedding—it is a reckoning. The Rapture is not depicted in these verses, but the return of Christ to the earth, where He separates the nations, as described later in the judgment of the sheep and goats (Matt. 25:31-46).

But Jesus Did Teach the Rapture — Elsewhere

While the Olivet Discourse primarily focuses on Israel and the Tribulation, Jesus did teach about the Rapture—just not in Matthew 24. We find it in John 14:1-3, where He offers personal comfort to His disciples:

> *"I go to prepare a place for you... I will come again and will take you to Myself, that where I am you may be also."*

This is bridal language that we discussed earlier. It aligns perfectly with Paul's teaching in 1 Thessalonians 4:17—that believers will be "caught up" to meet the Lord in the air and go to His prepared place. Jesus is not describing a return to earth to set up His kingdom here, but a removal of His people to dwell in His Father's house.

John 14 is the Rapture in seed form: a personal return, a heavenly destination, and a comforting hope—not a public return to judge the nations.

What About "Immediately After the Tribulation"?

Some point to Matthew 24:29-31, where Jesus says, "Immediately after the tribulation... He will send out His angels... and they will gather His elect," and argue that this proves a Post-Tribulational

Rapture.

But this is a different event. The elect here are not the Church; they are likely the redeemed of Israel and surviving Tribulation saints. The angels gather them for the inauguration of the Millennial Kingdom—not for glorification or removal.

There is no mention of the dead in Christ rising. No mention of transformation. No ascent into heaven. This is not the same gathering Paul describes in his letters to the Thessalonians and Corinthians.

"As It Was in the Days of Noah…"

Jesus gives a striking parallel to Noah in Matthew 24:37-39. In Noah's day, people were eating and drinking, marrying and living life—until the flood came and "swept them all away." The world was caught off guard. But Noah was removed from harm—lifted above judgment—while the wicked perished below.

This is the pattern of deliverance we've seen before: removal of the righteous before wrath. It is echoed in the lives of Enoch, Lot, and now Noah. This pattern reinforces, rather than challenges, the idea of a Pre-Tribulation Rapture.

What About Israel in Egypt?

Some critics argue, "But Israel stayed in Egypt during the plagues—couldn't God protect His people again during the Tribulation?" Yes, He could. And in fact, He will—but those people are not the Church.

During the Tribulation, we see 144,000 from the tribes of Israel sealed for protection (Revelation 7). Please note that these are 12,000 from each of the tribes of Israel. They are not Gentiles who have received Christ. We see a remnant of believing Jews preserved in the wilderness (Revelation 12:14). We see saints overcome yet redeemed—those "who came out of the great tribulation" (Rev. 7:14). Though to this I will add for the sake of clarity, those Israelites who come to receive the Messiah during the church age, are part of the Bride of Christ.

So yes, God preserves His people during judgment—but in every age, He does so according to His redemptive program. In Egypt, He preserved Israel, a nation not yet redeemed. In the Tribulation, He will again preserve Israel, as He fulfills His covenant promises.

But the Church is a different people, born of a different covenant. We are not preserved through wrath—we are removed before it.

The Olivet Discourse is not the Church's roadmap for the Rapture—it is Israel's warning for the Tribulation. Jesus will return for His Bride before the Day of the Lord begins. He will come again in glory after it ends. And between these two comings lies the greatest shaking the world has ever seen. But for the Church, the blessed hope remains that we will not be swept away in wrath—we will be lifted up in love.

Chapter 13

The Mystery of the Church and the Hidden Rapture

"Behold, I tell you a mystery: We shall not all sleep, but we shall all be changed…"

— 1 Corinthians 15:51

"…the mystery hidden for ages and generations but now revealed to his saints."

— Colossians 1:26

In Scripture, a "mystery" is not something unknowable it is something once concealed but now revealed by divine revelation. Mysteries are God's secrets, unveiled in their appointed time. And one of the greatest mysteries revealed in the New Testament is the Church itself, and with it, the sudden and supernatural event we now call the Rapture.

Understanding the concept of "mystery" is essential for rightly dividing the word of truth and recognizing the distinctions between Israel and the Church, between Old Testament prophecy and New Testament revelation, and between the Second Coming and the Rapture.

The Church Was Hidden

The Church — the Body of Christ, made up of Jew and Gentile in one spiritual union — was not revealed in the Old Testament. The prophets spoke of a coming Messiah, a suffering servant, a glorious king. They foresaw the regathering of Israel, the judgment of nations, and the reign of peace. But they did not see the Church Age.

This was intentional. As Paul wrote:

> *"This mystery was not made known to the sons of men in other generations... that the Gentiles are fellow heirs, members of the same body..."*

— Ephesians 3:5–6

The Church is not a continuation of Israel. It is a new creation, brought into being at Pentecost, indwelt by the Spirit, and commissioned to carry the gospel to the nations. The Church is Christ's Bride, not His kingdom subject. She is His partner in redemption, not simply a participant in judgment.

Because the Church was hidden in the Old Testament, so too was the Rapture — the unique and final event that concludes her time on earth.

The Rapture Is a Mystery Revealed

In 1 Corinthians 15:51, Paul introduces his teaching on the Rapture with these words: "Behold, I tell you a mystery." He is not drawing from the prophets. He is not quoting Daniel or Isaiah. He is unveiling something new — a truth not previously known, but now made clear through the Spirit.

The mystery is this: *"We shall not all sleep [die], but we shall all be changed...
in a moment, in the twinkling of an eye."*

This was not the resurrection at the end of the age that Martha
confessed in John 11. This was something different. This was the
sudden transformation of the living — an event distinct from the
resurrection of the dead. It is not found in the Gospels. It is not found
in Revelation's judgments. It is a mystery revealed through Paul, just as
the nature of the Church was.

Hidden Between the Hills

As we've discussed, prophetic vision often sees the peaks of history
but misses the valleys in between. The prophets saw the suffering
Messiah and the reigning King — but not the Church in between. They
saw judgment and restoration, but not an age of grace. They saw the
mountain of Calvary and the mountain of the Kingdom, but not the
valley of the cross-bearing Church.

This is why the Rapture is not described in the Olivet Discourse. Jesus
was speaking to Israel, about Israel. But Paul, writing to the Church,
unveils what had been hidden. The Rapture is not missing from
prophecy because it's unimportant — it's hidden because it belongs to
a mystery people, for a mystery moment, in God's mystery plan.

Mystery and the Timing of the Rapture

Mystery also implies imminence. There are no signs that must precede the Rapture. It is not tied to political treaties, abominations, or cosmic disturbances. It is tied only to the Father's timing and the completeness of the Church.

This is why Paul and the early believers lived in expectancy. They weren't wrong to believe Jesus could return in their day — they were right to remain ready. The Rapture is not a puzzle to be solved; it is a mystery to be embraced.

A Distinct Hope for a Distinct People

The Church has a unique relationship with Christ—and therefore a unique hope. Our calling is heavenly, not earthly. Our citizenship is above, not below. Our reward is a crown, not a kingdom on earth.

In Colossians 3:4, Paul writes:

"When Christ who is your life appears, then you also will appear with Him in

glory."

This is the Church's glorification. It is distinct from Israel's national restoration, distinct from the judgment of the nations, and distinct from the Millennial Kingdom. It is our blessed hope, and it is rooted in mystery.

The Church began with a supernatural event—the outpouring of the Holy Spirit. It will conclude with a supernatural event — the catching away of the Bride. The removal of the restrainer.

The Rapture was hidden for generations. It is the mystery that completes the mystery of the Church — not an interruption to prophecy, but an unveiling of grace. In a moment, the Bride will rise. And the age of mystery will give way to the age of fulfillment. The Church's work will be done. Her reward will be given. And the Bridegroom will receive His Bride.

Chapter 14

The Restrainer Removed: 2 Thessalonians and the Rise of the Lawless One

"For the mystery of lawlessness is already at work; only he who now restrains it will do so until he is taken out of the way. And then the lawless one will be revealed..."

— 2 Thessalonians 2:7-8

In every generation, believers have looked at the growing lawlessness around them and wondered, "How long, O Lord?" Why does evil persist? Why does injustice thrive? Why hasn't the Antichrist yet emerged on the global stage? Paul gives a clear, if cryptic, answer in 2 Thessalonians: there is a restrainer.

Something—someone—is actively holding back the rise of unfiltered evil. But the time is coming when that restraint will be removed. And when it is, the man of lawlessness will be revealed.

This passage is not only one of the most sobering in the New Testament—it's also one of the most clarifying. It explains why the Tribulation has not yet begun, why the Antichrist is still waiting in the wings, and why the Church must be removed first. **"You Know What** is Restraining Him Now"

Paul writes as though the Thessalonians already understood who or what the restrainer is. In verse 6, he says:

"You know what is restraining him now." This assumes prior teaching—likely from Paul's brief time with them (Acts 17:1–9).

Then, in verse 7, Paul switches to the personal: *"Only he who now restrains will do so until he is taken out of the way."*

Why the change? Because the restrainer is not just an impersonal force, like government or ideology. Nor is it just a message, like the gospel. It is a personal presence operating through a collective vessel: the Holy Spirit working through the Church.

This combination of neuter (what is restraining) and masculine (he who restrains) follows a known syntactical pattern in Greek. It often occurs when referring to the Holy Spirit, who, while technically neuter in gender (*to Pneuma*), is often spoken of with personal pronouns to emphasize His personhood (see John 14:26; 16:13-14).

This is not a grammatical accident—it is a theological fingerprint.

Why Not Government or Angels?

Some have proposed that the restrainer is the human government, based on Romans 13, or the archangel Michael, based on Daniel 12:1. Others argue that it is preaching, law, or conscience. But none of these interpretations hold up.

Human governments are often agents of evil, not preventers of it. And the rise of the Antichrist will occur within global government, not in its absence (Revelation 13:7). Michael, while a mighty angel, is not omnipresent and is only explicitly assigned to Israel, not the Church.

Only the Holy Spirit meets the criteria:

- Present from Pentecost to now

- Omnipresent yet personally active

- Powerful enough to suppress Satan's program

- Removed only when the Church is removed

The Church as the Spirit's Vessel

During this Church age, the Holy Spirit indwells believers corporately. We are His temple (1 Corinthians 3:16), His Body (1 Corinthians 12:13), and His witness on earth (Acts 1:8).

This role is distinct from the Spirit's Old Testament operations. In that era, He came *upon* individuals temporarily. But now, He dwells within all believers as a seal (Ephesians 1:13), a guarantee (2 Corinthians 1:22), and a restraining presence.

But when the Church is "caught up," the Spirit's restraining function is removed. Not because the Spirit is gone— He is eternal and omnipresent—but because His chosen vessel for restraint is no longer on earth.

This does not mean people won't be saved during the Tribulation.

Many will. But the unique, restraining presence of the Spirit through the corporate Body of Christ will be gone. The salt will have been removed. The light will be taken up.

The Revelation of the Man of Sin

Paul's wording is precise: *"Then the lawless one will be revealed."* The Antichrist is not revealed until this point. He may exist, he may rise politically, but his true identity is veiled until the restraint is lifted.

This again confirms a Pre-Tribulation framework:

- The Rapture occurs

- The restrainer is removed

- The Antichrist is revealed

- The Day of the Lord begins

This chronology undercuts any Post-Trib or Mid-Trib argument. If the Antichrist must be revealed before the Church is removed, then Paul's entire comfort to the Thessalonians makes no sense. The whole point of 2 Thessalonians 2 is to assure them they are not in the Day of the Lord, because that day cannot begin until the departure happens.

The Restraint of God Is Not Indifference — It's Mercy

Some might wonder: If the restraining force is the Spirit working through the Church, and if the world is clearly growing darker, then why hasn't the Rapture already happened? Why does God allow delay when the time seems ripe?

Peter gives us the answer in one of my favorite verses:

"The Lord is not slow about His promise, as some count slowness, but is patient toward you, not wishing for any to perish but for all to come to repentance."

— 2 Peter 3:9

God's restraint is not a sign of negligence—it is an act of mercy. He delays judgment not because He has forgotten His promise, but because He is still extending grace. Every moment the Restrainer remains is another moment for repentance. Every delay in His coming is another soul brought into the kingdom.

The Restrainer is not simply holding back evil; He is preserving the window of salvation. We live in that window now. But it will not remain open forever.

Just as Noah built the ark while God delayed the flood, the Church builds Christ's body while the Spirit holds back wrath. But the flood did come. And so will He.

The Rapture as a Catalyst

The departure of the Church is not just an exit — it is a divine trigger. It shifts the earth from the age of grace to the time of wrath. From spiritual invitation to eschatological judgment.

The Rapture is not merely our escape — it is God's declaration that the restraining time is over.

The Church, having fulfilled her commission, is removed. The Spirit, no longer operating in the same corporate, restraining function, ceases to hold back lawlessness. And in that vacuum, evil is given its hour.

The Antichrist will rise not in defiance of the Spirit, but in His absence. But even then, his days will be numbered.

When the Restrainer is removed, the man of sin will rise. However, his appearance will not catch the world off guard because God was slow to act — it will be because God was merciful in waiting. His delay is salvation. His patience is grace. But the day is coming when the restraining presence will be taken out of the way — not in defeat, but in triumph. For when the Bride is called home, her task is finished. And the curtain rises on the final act of redemption.

Chapter 15

Caught Up: The Word *Harpazō* and Its Biblical Meaning

*"Then we who are alive, who are left, will be **caught up** together with them in the clouds to meet the Lord in the air, and so we will always be with the Lord."*

— 1 Thessalonians 4:17

"Behold, I tell you a mystery: We shall not all sleep, but we shall all be changed—in a moment, in the twinkling of an eye..."

— 1 Corinthians 15:51-52

As we have discussed, the word *"rapture"* never appears in most English Bibles — and yet the concept is drawn directly from the inspired Greek text. In 1 Thessalonians 4:17, Paul writes that believers who are alive at the Lord's return will be "caught up" — and the Greek word used here is ἁρπάζω (*harpazo*). This single verb, full of power and immediacy, forms the foundation of what we now call the Rapture.

The term *"rapture"* comes from the Latin translation of this same verse — *rapiemur*, from the root *rapio*, meaning "to seize, snatch, or carry off suddenly." When the Latin Vulgate translated the Bible from

Greek, *"harpazo" became "rapiemur."* From this, the English word "rapture" was born.

But *harpazo* is more than just a semantic curiosity. It is a word that reveals the very character of the Rapture: sudden, forceful, decisive, and divine.

The Force of the Word

In the New Testament, harpazo is used 14 times, and each time it describes a violent or sudden act of seizing. It never implies a gradual or passive transition. It always denotes power. Consider a few examples:

- **John 10:28–29** – "No one will snatch them out of my hand." (harpazo)

- **Acts 8:39** – "The Spirit of the Lord caught up Philip, and the eunuch saw him no more."

- **2 Corinthians 12:2–4** – Paul describes being caught up to the third heaven — the same word.

- **Revelation 12:5** – The male child (symbolizing Christ) is caught up to God and His throne.

Each of these uses captures a supernatural, swift, and deliberate act of removal. It is not merely movement. It is rescue, transport, and dominion.

So when Paul uses *harpazo* to describe what will happen to living believers, he is not picturing a gentle fading into the sky. He is painting a picture of God's sovereign hand reaching into the world and forcibly claiming what is His.

The Rapture Is Not a Return — It's a Retrieval

One of the crucial distinctions in Rapture theology is that the Rapture is not the Second Coming. In the Second Coming, Jesus returns to the earth with His saints (Revelation 19:14).

However, in the Rapture, Jesus does not descend to the earth; instead, we ascend to meet Him in the air (1 Thessalonians 4:17).

The verb harpazo reinforces this. It is not Jesus landing and gathering people — it is Him calling and seizing them upward.

This event fulfills His promise in John 14:

"I will come again and will take you to myself, that where I am you may be also."

— (John 14:3)

Jesus is not returning to reign at this point — He is coming to receive His Bride, taking her out of the world before the Day of the Lord begins.

A Sudden and Irresistible Event

Paul elaborates on this in 1 Corinthians 15:52:

"In a moment, in the twinkling of an eye, at the last trumpet… the dead will be raised imperishable, and we shall be changed."

The word for "moment" here is ἄτομος (atomos) — literally, something indivisible, too fast to measure. The "twinkling of an eye" refers not to a blink, but to the flicker of light reflecting off the eye — a millisecond.

The Rapture is not something we can plan for or prepare for. It will be instantaneous, unavoidable, and completely transformational. We will be here one moment, and in the next, glorified and with the Lord.

This is in perfect alignment with harpazo — a sudden snatching, not a slow ascent.

The Harpazo and Rescue Motif

Throughout Scripture, harpazo also carries the idea of deliverance from danger. In Jude 23, believers are told to "snatch others from the fire" — a life-saving intervention. In Revelation 12:5, the male child is caught up to safety before the dragon can harm him.

The Rapture fits this same pattern. The Church is not simply going to meet her Lord — she is being removed before the wrath to come.

As Paul writes: *"Jesus who delivers us from the wrath to come."*

— 1 Thessalonians 1:10

The harpazo is not an escape from tribulation in general (which the Church has always endured), but from the unique, global wrath of God poured out during the Tribulation (Revelation 6–19).

It's Not Just About Leaving — It's About Belonging

Harpazo is also about possession. In John 10, Jesus says no one can *snatch* His sheep from His hand. The word conveys a deep sense of ownership and security.

When Christ *harpazoes* His Church, He declares to heaven and earth, "These are mine."

The Rapture is not only about being taken from earth — it is about being taken to Him. It is not merely the end of one chapter; it is the beginning of another: the Marriage of the Lamb, the Bema Seat of Christ, and ultimately, our eternal union with the Bridegroom.

Paul closes his description of the Rapture with these words:

> *"Therefore encourage one another with these words."*

> — 1 Thessalonians 4:18

And no wonder. There is nothing in this world more comforting than knowing that our Lord is not slow. He is not absent. He is waiting for the right moment — the appointed hour to reach down and snatch us up, forever out of reach of wrath, sorrow, and sin.

The Rapture is not a soft departure. It is a sudden act of divine power. One moment we are ambassadors in enemy territory. The next, we are caught up — claimed, changed, and crowned. Harpazo is not just a word; it is the cry of a King, the hand of the Bridegroom, and the final punctuation mark on the age of grace.

Chapter 16

The Marriage of the Lamb and the Bema Seat of Christ

"Let us rejoice and exult and give Him the glory, for the marriage of the Lamb has come, and His Bride has made herself ready…"

— Revelation 19:7

"For we must all appear before the judgment seat of Christ…"

— 2 Corinthians 5:10

If the Rapture is the catching away of the Bride, then what follows is the consummation of that relationship in heaven: the Marriage of the Lamb, and the rewarding of the saints at the Bema Seat of Christ. These two events are distinct, but deeply intertwined. One reveals the love of Christ; the other, His perfect justice. Both are promises fulfilled — and together they define the heavenly purpose for which the Rapture exists.

A Marriage Foretold

All throughout Scripture, God uses the language of marriage to describe His relationship with His people. In the Old Testament, Israel is often pictured as God's unfaithful wife (Jeremiah 3:20; Hosea 2:2).

In the New Testament, the Church is revealed not merely as a people, but as a Bride — pure, beloved, and betrothed to Christ.

"I betrothed you to one husband, to present you as a pure virgin to Christ."

— 2 Corinthians 11:2

And where there is betrothal, there must be wedding. Jesus Himself spoke of it in parables (Matt. 22:2-14; Matt. 25:1- 13). John the Baptist referred to Christ as the Bridegroom (John 3:29). And the book of Revelation culminates in a wedding:

"Blessed are those who are invited to the marriage supper of the Lamb."

— Revelation 19:9

The Marriage of the Lamb is not symbolic poetry. It is the literal, heavenly celebration of Christ and His Church — a union that began in promise and is completed in presence.

The Jewish Wedding Pattern

To fully understand the imagery, it helps to look at the ancient Jewish wedding tradition, which unfolds in three key stages — each of which has a prophetic fulfillment in Christ's relationship with the Church:

1. **Betrothal** – This was a binding covenant, initiated by the groom. The bride was set apart and sealed, awaiting the day of union.

— This parallels our salvation and the indwelling of the Holy Spirit (Eph. 1:13-14).

2. Fetching the Bride – At an unknown hour, the groom would come and take his bride to the father's house, often with a shout and trumpet.

— This parallels the Rapture (1 Thess. 4:16-17; John 14:1-3).

3. Marriage Supper – A great feast would follow, celebrating the union of the couple.

— This parallels the Marriage Supper of the Lamb (Revelation 19:7-9).

Jesus follows this pattern perfectly. He has betrothed His Church, promised to return, and will one day soon catch her away — not merely to escape judgment, but to celebrate eternal union with Him.

The Bema Seat of Christ

Before the Marriage Supper occurs, another event takes place: the Judgment Seat of Christ, also called the Bema Seat.

"For we must all appear before the judgment seat of Christ, so that each one may receive what is due for what he has done in the body, whether good or evil."

— 2 Corinthians 5:10

This is not a judgment of condemnation (Romans 8:1), but of evaluation and reward. The Greek word bēma refers to a raised platform where prizes were awarded in athletic contests — such as the Olympics. It was a place of honor, not punishment.

At the Bema Seat, Christ will examine the works of believers — not to determine salvation, but to reward faithfulness.

"Each one's work will become manifest... and the fire will test what sort of work each one has done. If the work... survives, he will receive a reward."

— 1 Corinthians 3:13-14

Some will receive crowns (2 Tim. 4:8; James 1:12). Others will suffer loss — not of salvation, but of reward (1 Cor. 3:15). It is a moment of holy accountability. Every hidden motive will be brought to light. Every act of obedience, every sacrifice, every tear shed in His name — all remembered, all repaid.

Not All Will Receive the Same

The Bema Seat reminds us that grace is free, but reward is earned. Not all believers will shine equally in the Kingdom. Some will rule over ten cities, while others will rule over five (Luke 19:17-19). Some will be crowned, others bare-headed. Yet all will be saved, and all will rejoice.

What matters now is how we live, what we build with — gold, silver, and precious stones, or wood, hay, and stubble. The Rapture removes us from the earth; the Bema Seat reveals what we did while we were here.

The Timing

The sequence is important. The Rapture brings the Church to Christ. The Bema Seat follows, where rewards are distributed. Then, adorned and crowned, the Bride enters the Marriage Supper of the Lamb (Rev. 19:7-9).

This order reinforces the purpose of the Rapture: not just to escape wrath, but to enter joy. Not just to be spared judgment, but to be prepared for glory.

The Rapture is the beginning of union. The Bema Seat is the revealing of works. The Marriage is the celebration of love fulfilled. In these heavenly moments, we see the full arc of redemption completed: betrothed by grace, caught up by promise, rewarded by faithfulness, and wed to the Lamb forever. This is our hope. This is our destiny. And this is why the Church says, "Come, Lord Jesus."

Chapter 17

The Church's Dual Citizenship:
Ambassadors Before the King Returns

"But our citizenship is in heaven, and from it we await a Savior, the Lord Jesus Christ…"

— Philippians 3:20

"Therefore, we are ambassadors for Christ, God making His appeal through us."

— 2 Corinthians 5:20

Why hasn't the Rapture already happened? Why does the Church remain in a world that increasingly rejects truth, embraces lawlessness, and marches toward judgment? If we are the Bride of Christ, already betrothed, already sealed by the Spirit, why does He delay?

The answer is not uncertainty, weakness, or oversight. It is intentionality. It is mercy, and it is mission.

Citizens of Heaven, Residents on Earth

The moment someone believes in Christ, they are born again — spiritually regenerated, sealed by the Holy Spirit, and given eternal life. But they are not immediately removed from the world. Instead, they are left here for a purpose. And in that tension, a new identity emerges: dual citizenship.

Paul tells us that our true citizenship is in heaven (Phil. 3:20). Yet we still walk, breathe, and live on earth — not as passive passengers, but as active representatives.

We are not of this world — but we are still in it. We are no longer under its authority — but we are called to impact it.

This tension is not a mistake. It is a calling. God has placed His redeemed people in the middle of enemy territory, not to be consumed by it, but to shine within it.

Ambassadors of the Coming Kingdom

Paul uses the language of ambassadorship in 2 Corinthians 5. An ambassador is someone who resides in a foreign country, representing the interests of their home country.

He carries the authority, message, and character of the king who sent him.

That is who the Church is. We represent heaven in a fallen world. We don't speak for ourselves — we speak for the King. Our lives, our words, and our love are all part of God's appeal to the world through us:

"Be reconciled to God."

— (2 Cor. 5:20)

This is the mission of the Church in the age of grace: to extend the invitation of salvation before judgment comes. Just as Noah preached before the flood, and just as Lot lingered before Sodom burned, we remain as messengers of mercy.

Why the Rapture Hasn't Happened Yet

The delay of the Rapture is not divine indecision — it is divine compassion. As we saw earlier:

"The Lord is not slow about His promise, as some count slowness, but is patient toward you, not wishing for any to perish but for all to come to repentance."

— 2 Peter 3:9

The Spirit continues to restrain. The Bride continues to witness. The Gospel continues to go out. And the door of salvation remains open — for now.

We are the hands and feet of Jesus in this present age. We are the light of the world and the salt of the earth. The Rapture will come — but until then, the Church's task is not to retreat in fear, but to stand in faith.

Living Between Two Worlds

This is perhaps the greatest tension of the Christian life: we are already citizens of heaven, yet we suffer, grieve, and wrestle in a broken world. But this tension is the soil of sanctification.

We groan, as Paul says in Romans 8 — longing for the redemption of our bodies. And yet, in that very groaning, we grow in endurance, in hope, and in character.

We are not saved from suffering; we are sustained through it. The promise of Rapture is not an excuse for passivity — it is motivation for perseverance.

Because the King is coming, we proclaim. Because judgment is near, we warn. Because grace is still offered, we preach.

Holding Fast Until He Comes

The Church is not a social club or a survival shelter. It is a living Body, empowered by the Spirit, sent on mission by the Son. We are ambassadors, yes — but we are also watchmen, standing on the wall, declaring the coming of the King.

"Occupy until I come."

— Luke 19:13 (KJV)

The time is short. The world is dark. But the Bride still remains. And until the trumpet sounds, we are to stand, shine, speak, and serve.

The Rapture is coming — but until then, we remain on assignment. We are not forgotten; we are commissioned. We are not abandoned; we are appointed. As ambassadors of the Kingdom, our lives declare two realities: judgment is near, and grace is still offered. And when our mission is complete, when the last soul is sealed, the King will come for His Bride — and the Church's earthly chapter will close in glory.

Chapter 18

The Second Coming: With the Saints in Power

"Behold, He is coming with the clouds, and every eye will see Him…"

— Revelation 1:7

"And the armies of heaven, arrayed in fine linen, white and pure, were following Him on white horses."

— Revelation 19:14

At the Rapture, Christ comes like a thief in the night — sudden, unseen by the world. He comes for His Bride, and only the redeemed hear the trumpet. But at the Second Coming, it is altogether different. He comes with His saints, in blazing glory, and every eye will see Him. This return is not about rescue — it is about rule.

The Second Coming is the long-awaited culmination of prophecy, judgment, and justice. Evil will no longer be restrained it will be confronted. And the King of Kings will descend, not in humility, but in power and vengeance.

The Second Coming Is Not the Rapture

Though many confuse the two, Scripture makes clear that the Rapture and the Second Coming are distinct events with distinct purposes:

Rapture	Second Coming
Christ comes for His Church	Christ comes with His Church
Occurs before the Tribulation	Occurs after the Tribulation
Only believers see Him (1 Thess. 4:17)	Every eye will see Him (Rev. 1:7)
A message of comfort (1 Thess. 4:18)	A moment of judgment (Rev. 19)
Happens in the air	Happens on earth, at the Mount of Olives (Zech. 14:4)

The Rapture is private and protective. The Second Coming is a public and confrontational event. One removes the saints; the other defeats the wicked.

With the Armies of Heaven

John's vision in Revelation 19 depicts Christ descending on a white horse, crowned with many diadems, His robe stained with blood. But He is not alone:

"The armies of heaven, arrayed in fine linen, white and pure, were following Him on white horses."

— Revelation 19:14

Who are these armies? They are not angels alone. The white linen matches the description of the Bride of Christ just a few verses earlier (Revelation 19:8). These are the redeemed saints, returning with their Lord.

This is the Church — already raptured, already judged at the Bema Seat, already united with Christ — now returning to reign with Him.

"When Christ, who is your life appears, then you also will appear with Him in glory."

— Colossians 3:4

"Behold, the Lord comes with ten thousands of His holy ones, to execute judgment on all..."

— Jude 14–15

This is the fulfillment of victory. The Church, once a suffering servant on earth, now rides in victory. The Bride becomes the army. The ambassador becomes the ruler.

The Winepress of God's Wrath

The purpose of Christ's Second Coming is not rescue, but retribution. The Antichrist, the false prophet, and all who have taken the mark of the beast are gathered to war against Him (Rev. 19:19). But there is no battle — only defeat.

"From His mouth comes a sharp sword... He will tread the winepress of the fury of the wrath of God Almighty."

— Revelation 19:15

This imagery — the winepress — hearkens back to Isaiah 63, where the Messiah alone treads the winepress, staining His garments with the blood of His enemies. This is the moment of physical victory, just as the Cross won and the Rapture marked spiritual victory. One redeems the soul, the other redeems the earth.

The kingdoms of this world become the Kingdom of our Lord. Babylon falls. The Beast is cast into the lake of fire. Satan is bound. And Christ establishes His throne.

The Completion of Martyrdom

And yet, even this moment of judgment reveals the patience and precision of God. Back in Revelation 6:11, under the fifth seal, the martyrs cry out for justice:

"They were told to rest a little while longer, until the number of their fellow servants and their brethren who were to be killed even as they had been, would be completed also."

This is a stunning verse. It shows that:

— God has a sovereign plan, down to the number of martyrs.

— The delay of judgment is not weakness — it is mercy.

— Justice comes only when the plan is complete. At the Second Coming, that plan is fulfilled. The number is reached. The delay ends. The enemies of God are judged, and the prayer of the martyrs — *"How long, O Lord?"* — is answered once and for all.

The King Returns

Jesus came the first time in humility — born in a manger, riding on a donkey, crowned with thorns. But the second time, He comes as a conquering King — crowned with diadems, riding in glory, speaking a word that slays nations.

He comes not to take sides — He comes to take over.

And the Church will be there, not as bystanders, but as participants. We who were caught up in secret will now return in triumph. The Lamb is also the Lion.

The Rapture refers to Christ's coming for His Bride. The Second Coming is Christ returning with His army. One removes the righteous before wrath. The other delivers wrath upon the wicked. Together, they reveal a King who is both Savior and Judge, Lamb and Lion, Bridegroom and Warrior. The Church rejoices in both — for in each, Christ is glorified.

Chapter 19

The Millennial Reign and the Fulfillment of Promises to Israel

"Then I saw thrones, and seated on them were those to whom the authority to judge was committed... They came to life and reigned with Christ for a thousand years."

— Revelation 20:4

"And the Lord will be King over all the earth. On that day the Lord will be one and His name one."

— Zechariah 14:9

When Christ returns to earth in glory at the Second Coming, He does not simply end evil — He begins a reign. And it is not a symbolic, spiritual reign from heaven, but a literal, political, and visible reign upon the earth. This is what Scripture calls the Millennial Kingdom — a thousand-year period of righteousness, peace, and restoration under the rule of Jesus Christ.

This is no allegory. It is the fulfillment of ancient prophecy, covenants, and prayers. The Kingdom of God on earth long-awaited, long-promised — finally breaks through the veil.

A Thousand-Year Reign

Six times in Revelation 20, the phrase *"a thousand years"* is used to describe the duration of this reign. This is not poetic language. The repetition is intentional and emphatic. This is the first resurrection, the rule of the saints, and the final stage of redemptive history before eternity.

> *"They came to life and reigned with Christ for a thousand years."*

— Revelation 20:4

> *"The rest of the dead did not come to life until the thousand years were completed."*

— Revelation 20:5

This thousand-year reign includes:

— Christ physically ruling from Jerusalem

— The glorified saints sharing in His rule

— Satan bound and sealed in the abyss

— The nations at peace and creation restored

It is the direct and visible answer to the prayer, *"Thy kingdom come, Thy will be done, on earth as it is in heaven."*

Prophetic Pattern: Six Days and the Seventh

There is something even deeper at work beneath the text a pattern established by God Himself in creation.

"By the seventh day God completed His work which He had done, and He rested…"

—   Genesis 2:2

Early Christian writers noticed this pattern and began to see in it a prophetic structure. Most notably, Barnabas, Paul's companion, wrote in the *Epistle of Barnabas* (ca. 70–130 AD):

"With the Lord one day is as a thousand years. Therefore, children, in six days — that is, in six thousand years — all things will be completed. And on the seventh day He will rest… when His Son returns and destroys the time of the lawless one…"

— (Barnabas 15)

This idea found traction in the writings of Irenaeus, Lactantius, and others in the early Church. It goes like this:

— Six days of creation → 6,000 years of human history

— Seventh day of rest → 1,000-year reign of Christ

— "A day with the Lord is as a thousand years" (2 Peter 3:8) becomes the interpretive key

According to this model:

— The world experiences ~4,000 years from Adam to Christ

— ~2,000 years from Christ to the present Church Age

— Bringing us near the end of six millennia

— The seventh "day", the Millennium, is about to dawn — a Sabbath rest for the earth

This is not date-setting, but pattern recognition. It reveals the structural beauty of God's plan, mirroring creation itself. Hebrews 4:9 hints at this:

> *"There remains a Sabbath rest for the people of God."*

And what better Sabbath could there be than the age when the Prince of Peace reigns, justice is administered, creation is renewed, and the curse is rolled back?

Fulfillment of Promises to Israel

The Millennium also marks the fulfillment of God's irrevocable promises — especially to Israel.

To Abraham, God promised a land and descendants:

> *"To your descendants I have given this land…"*

> — Genesis 15:18

To David, He promised an eternal throne:

> *"Your house and your kingdom shall be established forever."*

> — 2 Samuel 7:16

The prophets were saturated with visions of this future:

— Isaiah spoke of a righteous reign and a renewed Jerusalem.

— Ezekiel foresaw the construction of a new temple and the

distribution of tribal inheritance.

— Zechariah described Israel mourning the One they pierced, then living under His reign.

These are not spiritual abstractions. They are ethnic, national, and territorial promises made to Israel. They have never been fulfilled in history — but they will be during the Millennium.

Paul affirms in Romans 11 that "all Israel will be saved," and that the "gifts and calling of God are irrevocable."

The Millennium is God's vindication — not just of His holiness and power, but of His faithfulness to a people often rejected, yet never forgotten.

The Church's Role in the Kingdom

While the Millennium centers on Israel's restoration, the Church — already glorified — is not passive. Revelation 20:4 tells us:

"They came to life and reigned with Christ…"

This includes:

— Raptured saints (Church Age believers)

— Tribulation martyrs

— Old Testament faithful

We will serve as co-regents under Christ. Jesus told His disciples that they would sit on thrones, judging the tribes of Israel (Matt. 19:28).

Paul said that we would judge angels and reign with Him (2 Tim. 2:12).

The Church is Christ's Body — and where the Head goes, the Body follows. We reign not in arrogance, but as witnesses of grace, reflecting the justice and mercy of the King.

The Conditions of the Kingdom

The world will look radically different during the Millennium:

— Satan is bound (Rev. 20:2)

— War ceases (Isa. 2:4)

— Longevity is restored (Isa. 65:20)

— Peace extends to nature itself (Isa. 11:6–9)

— Worship flows to Jerusalem (Zech. 14:16)

Though sin remains in those born during this time, justice is swift and righteousness is the law of the land. Christ rules with a rod of iron, but also with wounded hands.

The Final Rebellion and Judgment

After a thousand years, Satan is briefly released.

Astonishingly, many from among the nations choose to rebel — proving that even paradise cannot change the heart unless it is born again.

This final revolt is crushed instantly. Fire falls. The devil is thrown into the lake of fire forever. And history, as we know it, ends.

The Millennial Reign: Rest and Reign

The Millennium is not just a future curiosity — it is a necessary completion of God's plan:

— Redemption is vindicated

— Israel is restored

— The Church is glorified

— The earth is renewed

— Satan's defeat is finalized

It is the seventh day of God's redemptive week — the great Sabbath of peace, the cosmic rest before the eternal kingdom begins.

God created the world in six days and rested on the seventh. He has allowed humanity to rule for six thousand years and soon, the seventh day will dawn. The Millennial Kingdom is that rest: a time of healing, justice, and rule under Christ the King. It is not the end — but it is the preview of eternity. It is Eden restored, Israel redeemed, and the Bride reigning beside her King.

Chapter 20

The Eternal State: A New Heaven and a New Earth

"Then I saw a new heaven and a new earth, for the first heaven and the first earth had passed away…"

— Revelation 21:1

"Behold, the tabernacle of God is among men, and He will dwell among them…"

— Revelation 21:3

With the defeat of Satan, the end of the Millennial Kingdom, and the final judgment completed, the redemptive story of Scripture reaches its breathtaking conclusion. Everything that was broken is made new. Everything that was temporary is swallowed up by eternity. What began in a garden ends in a city but a city unlike any the world has ever seen. This is the eternal state: God dwelling with man, in perfect righteousness, forever.

A New Heaven and a New Earth

The apostle John's words are simple, but world-shaking:

"I saw a new heaven and a new earth…"

This is not merely a cleaned-up version of the old world. The word used for "new" (Greek *kainos*) signifies new in kind and quality — not merely new in time (*neos*). The former creation — marred by sin, stained by rebellion, groaning under the curse — is unmade to give way to a perfected order, one that can host God's unveiled presence.

"The first heaven and the first earth passed away…"

— (Rev. 21:1)

This echoes Peter's vision:

"The heavens will pass away with a roar… the earth and its works will be burned up… But according to His promise we are looking for new heavens and a new earth, in which righteousness dwells."

— 2 Peter 3:10–13

This is not annihilation, but purification through transformation — just as the resurrection body is not a replacement of our corpse but a glorified version of it. So too the cosmos is reborn — not destroyed, but transfigured.

The New Jerusalem

Descending from heaven comes the holy city, the New Jerusalem, prepared as a bride adorned for her husband. This is not merely a place — it is a picture of God's people made perfect, and a literal dwelling place where heaven and earth meet.

John describes its dimensions, its beauty, and its mystery:

— 12 foundations named after the apostles

— 12 gates named after the tribes of Israel

— Walls of jasper, streets of gold, and foundations of every precious stone

— A cubed city — its shape a perfect echo of the Most Holy Place in the Tabernacle (cf. 1 Kings 6:20)

It is as if the entire city is the Holy of Holies — because now God dwells with man fully and forever.

"I saw no temple in it, for the Lord God Almighty and the Lamb are its temple."

— Revelation 21:22

There is no sun or moon, because the glory of God illuminates it. There is no night, no death, no mourning, no crying, no pain. The former things — the long night of sorrow — have passed away.

God with Us

This is the deepest longing of Scripture:

"And I heard a loud voice from the throne saying, 'Behold, the dwelling place of God is with man.'"

— Revelation 21:3

What was lost in Eden is now restored — and even exceeded. In Eden, God walked with man in the cool of the day. Here, He dwells among them continually.

The Lamb who was slain now reigns without rivals. His Bride — the Church, completed and glorified — lives with Him in unmarred intimacy. The nations are healed. The curse is broken. The river of life flows freely. And the tree of life, once guarded by angels, is now accessible to all who are His.

Eternity Begins

There is no more sin, no more testing, no more enemy. The devil, the beast, the false prophet — all have been judged and cast into the lake of fire. Death itself is dead. Time, as we know it, gives way to eternity.

"They will see His face, and His name will be on their foreheads..."

— Revelation 22:4

We will reign with Him forever and ever — not floating as disembodied spirits, but as glorified beings in a renewed physical reality, where the spiritual and the material are in perfect harmony.

The eternal state is not the "end of the story" — it is the beginning of unending glory. Creation has been redeemed. Israel has been restored. The Church has been glorified. And God is all in all.

The Final Invitation

The last chapter of Revelation closes not with an argument, but an invitation:

"The Spirit and the bride say, 'Come.' And let the one who hears say, 'Come.'"

— Revelation 22:17

The door is still open. The story is still being written. The Church, as the Bride of Christ, extends the invitation to all who will come — before the age of grace closes and the King returns.

The Consummation of All Things

In the sweep of redemptive history — from Genesis to Revelation — we see the perfect arc of God's purposes:

In the Beginning	In the End
Heaven and earth created	New heaven and new earth
Garden of Eden	City of God
Tree of knowledge forbidden	Tree of life accessible
Man hides from God	Man sees His face
Curse begins	Curse ends
Death enters	Death is destroyed
Satan tempts	Satan is judged

Everything broken is mended. Everything lost is found.

Every promise is fulfilled.

He who testifies to these things says, "Yes, I am coming quickly."

Amen. Come, Lord Jesus.

— Revelation 22:20

Chapter 21

A Sound Doctrine Confirmed

As we end this study, it is right and necessary to pause— not to rehearse what we've already said, but to ask with honesty: *Have we truly made the case? Have we faithfully and clearly demonstrated that the pre-tribulation rapture is the view most consistent with Scripture itself?* To which I would reply, read through the evidence again.

That is, after all, what this journey has been about. Not theological novelty. Not denominational loyalty. But truth. Truth grounded in God's Word. Truth that doesn't bend to fear or tradition or academic trends—but bows only to what is written. And the answer to that question is: yes, we have.

The pre-tribulation rapture view is not just plausible; it is, when Scripture is read carefully, humbly, and in its full prophetic scope, the only model that preserves the integrity of God's promises, the chronology of prophecy, the hope of the Church, and the redemptive plan for Israel.

Not Just the Best View — the Only One That Holds

Alternative frameworks certainly exist. The post- tribulation model posits that the Rapture and the Second Coming are one and the same event. The mid-tribulation or pre-wrath views position the rapture later in the Tribulation, aiming to strike a balance between warning and hope. Amillennial and symbolic systems dismiss the entire timeline, seeing Revelation as metaphor.

But each of these systems, when held to the light of Scripture, collapses under close inspection.

The post-tribulation view denies the imminency Jesus taught. It erases the distinction between Israel and the Church. It cannot explain how believers enter the Millennial Kingdom in mortal bodies if all saints are glorified at His coming. Nor can it reconcile the "coming like a thief" with the countdown of clear, terrifying signs.

The mid-trib and pre-wrath views, though well-meaning, rely on ambiguous distinctions between God's wrath and Satan's activity. They retain many of the same inconsistencies of the post-tribulation view and still undermine the doctrine of any- moment expectation.

The symbolic or amillennial views go even further. They do not simply adjust the timeline—they erase it. They spiritualize the literal. They reassign Israel's promises to the Church. And in doing so, they lose the texture of God's covenants, the beauty of typology, and the faithfulness of the God who keeps His word to the letter.

Why This Matters

The pre-tribulation rapture view:

— Preserves imminency — Jesus can return at any moment

— Delivers the Church from wrath — in line with 1 Thessalonians 1:10 and Revelation 3:10

— Upholds the distinction between Israel and the Church — as Daniel 9:24 requires

— Honors the structure of prophetic Scripture — without allegorizing what God intended literally

— Protects the consistency of God's character — in dealing with different peoples, covenants, and promises

— Gives coherent hope — without confusion or contradiction

It is the only framework that explains the removal of the restrainer before the revealing of the man of sin. The only view that accounts for the typology of Noah and Lot. The only view that fits the "twinkling of an eye" catching up and the simultaneous return of Christ with His saints. The only view that allows for both spiritual victory (at the rapture) and physical victory (at the return).

But the Greatest Proof Is This:

"God has not destined us for wrath, but to obtain salvation through our Lord Jesus Christ."

— (1 Thess. 5:9)

"Because you have kept My command to endure, I will also keep you from the hour of trial that is coming upon the whole world."

— (Rev. 3:10)

"When these things begin to take place... lift up your heads, for your redemption draws near."

— (Luke 21:28)

The text speaks for itself. Again and again.

We Are Not Escaping — We Are Awaiting

This doctrine does not breed passivity. It does not breed arrogance. It breeds hope and holiness. It keeps the Bride ready. It keeps the lamp burning. It keeps the ambassador at his post.

We are not looking for the Antichrist — we are looking for Jesus Christ. The One who promised:

"I go to prepare a place for you... I will come again and take you to Myself, that where I am, you may be also."

—   (John 14:3)

And as we wait, we work. We witness. We worship. We remember that we are not appointed to judgment — but to glory.

We remember that we are already spiritually seated with Christ — and we are soon to be physically united with Him as well.

And if there's still one reason why we're here — it is this:

"The Lord is not slow to fulfill His promise... but is patient toward you, not wishing that any should perish."

— (2 Peter 3:9)

So we preach. We pray. We endure. And we look up. Because the fig

135

tree has sprouted. The trumpet is near. The Groom is ready.

Come, Lord Jesus. Your Bride is watching. Your Word is true.

Your hour is at hand.

BIBLIOGRAPHY

Bible Translations

The Holy Bible: English Standard Version. Wheaton, IL: Crossway, 2016.

The Holy Bible: King James Version. Cambridge Edition. Public Domain.

Tyndale, William. *The Tyndale Bible (1526)*. London: Public Domain Edition.

The Geneva Bible (1560). London: Public Domain Edition.

Early Church Writings and Typology

Barnabas. *The Epistle of Barnabas*. In *The Ante-Nicene Fathers*, Vol. 1. Translated by Alexander Roberts and James Donaldson. Buffalo, NY: Christian Literature Publishing Co., 1885.

Hippolytus. *On Christ and Antichrist*. In *The Ante-Nicene Fathers*, Vol. 5. Translated by J. H. MacMahon. Buffalo, NY: Christian Literature Publishing Co., 1886.

Irenaeus. *Against Heresies*. In *The Ante-Nicene Fathers*, Vol. 1. Translated by Alexander Roberts and James Donaldson. Buffalo, NY: Christian Literature Publishing Co., 1885.

Justin Martyr. *Dialogue with Trypho*. In *The Ante-Nicene Fathers*, Vol. 1.

Translated by Alexander Roberts and James Donaldson. Buffalo, NY: Christian Literature Publishing Co., 1885.

Scholarly and Prophetic Studies

Anderson, Robert. *The Coming Prince*. London: Hodder & Stoughton, 1895.

Doukhan, Jacques B. "The Seventy Weeks of Dan 9: An Exegetical Study." *Andrews University Seminary Studies* 17, no. 1 (1979): 1–22.

Gurney, Robert J. M. "The Seventy Weeks of Daniel 9:24–27." *Evangelical Quarterly* 53, no. 1 (1981): 29–37.

Haynes, J. L. *Interpreting the Vision: The 70 Weeks of Daniel*. Unpublished manuscript, 2004.

Hoehner, Harold W. *Chronological Aspects of the Life of Christ*. Grand Rapids, MI: Zondervan, 1977.

Jarrett, Nathaniel. *"Correcting Harold Hoehner's Interpretation of Daniel's 70 Weeks."* Eleutheria 5, no. 1 (2021): 46–65.

Johnson, Matt. *An Exegetical Report on Daniel 9:24–27*. Dallas Theological Seminary, 2022.

Ngai, Hing Gavin. "Re-Examining and Re-Interpreting the 70 Weeks Prophecy: A Historicist Evaluation." *Biblical Studies Journal* 19, no. 2 (2022): 149–196.

Pierce, Ronald W. "Spiritual Failure, Postponement, and Daniel 9." *Trinity Journal* 10, no. 1 (1989): 61–72.

Tanner, J. Paul. "Is Daniel's Seventy-Weeks Prophecy Messianic? Part 1: The Historical and Cultural Context." *Bibliotheca Sacra* 166 (January–March 2009): 18–33.—— "Part 2: The Chronological Aspects." *Bibliotheca Sacra* 166 (April–June 2009): 197–216.

Gunn, Glen. *"Daniel 9:24–27 – The Seventy Heptads."* Shasta Bible College Lecture Notes, 2010.

Jewish Calendar & Chronology

Chabad.org – Jewish Calendar Resources. https://www.chabad.org/calendar

Hebcal.com – Jewish Date Converter. https://www.hebcal.com

Seder Olam Rabbah. Ancient Jewish Chronology. As cited in various rabbinic sources.

Additional Typological and Theological References

The Holy Bible. Scripture references are drawn from the ESV, KJV, and Tyndale translations.

Paul the Apostle. *The Epistle to the Romans* and *The Epistle to the Galatians.* Used typologically regarding Isaac, Ishmael, Jacob, and Esau.

www.ingramcontent.com/pod-product-compliance
Lightning Source LLC
Chambersburg PA
CBHW051207120626
46547CB00013B/1246